KIVALINA

A CLIMATE CHANGE STORY

Christine Shearer

Haymarket Books
Chicago, Illinois

First published by Haymarket Books in 2011
© 2011 Christine Shearer

Haymarket Books
P.O. Box 180165
Chicago, IL 60618
773-583-7884
info@haymarketbooks.org
www.haymarketbooks.org

ISBN: 978-1-60846-128-8

Trade distribution:
In the U.S., Consortium Book Sales and Distribution, www.cbsd.com
In Canada, Publishers Group Canada, www.pgcbooks.ca
In the UK, Turnaround Publisher Services, www.turnaround-uk.com
In Australia, Palgrave Macmillan, www.palgravemacmillan.com.au
All other countries, Publishers Group Worldwide, www.pgw.com

Cover design by Amy Balkan.

Cover image by Tim Matsui: May 3, 2008—Kivalina, Alaska, U.S.A. A ready whaling boat sits on the edge of the sea ice, as native Inupiat wait to spot a beluga or bowhead whale some two miles out on the melting sea ice, twelve miles from the native village of Kivalina, Alaska.

Special discounts are available for bulk purchases by organizations and institutions. Please contact Haymarket Books for more information at 773-583-7884 or info@haymarketbooks.org.

This book was published with the generous support of the Lannan Foundation and the Wallace Global Fund.

Printed in Canada by union labor on recycled paper containing 100 percent post-consumer waste in accordance with the guidelines of the Green Press Initiative, www.greenpressinitiative.org

Library of Congress CIP Data is available

2 4 6 8 10 9 7 5 3 1

PRAISE FOR *KIVALINA*

"This story is a tragedy, and not just because of what's happening to the people of Kivalina. It's a tragedy because it's unnecessary—the product, as the author shows, of calculation, deception, manipulation, and greed on the part of some of the biggest and richest companies on earth."

—Bill McKibben, author of *Eaarth: Making a Life on a Tough New Planet*

"I watched the lights of the oil fields grow in intensity and proximity, although they were many miles away. The flaring of the gas became a harbinger of hard nights on call, due to increases in respiratory illness among our people. Compounding this were changes to the land and water around us, affecting the animals and their [habits].... This book provides an understanding of the obstacles I have been facing while working on the basic issues of promoting and protecting the health, culture, and traditions of our people."

—Rosemary Ahtuanguaruak, board member of the Inupiat Community of the Arctic Slope, founding member of REDOIL (Resisting Environmental Destruction on Indigenous Lands), and community health practitioner

"Christine Shearer's *Kivalina: A Climate Change Story* is a fast and bumpy ride that begins with the history of outrageous corporate deceptions through public relations and legal campaigns, continuing with the building of the coal-and-oil empire to fuel progress in the United States, leading to the horrendous politics of climate crisis, and finally arriving at its destination—a ground zero of climate refugees, Kivalina, an Inupiat community along the Chukchi Sea coast of Arctic Alaska. I was angry when I turned the last page. I urge you to get a copy, read it, share the story, and join the global climate justice movement."

—Subhankar Banerjee, writer, activist, and photographer of *Arctic National Wildlife Refuge: Seasons of Life and Land*

"The climate catastrophe is real and growing, and this is the story of some of its first known victims, with many millions more to follow. This is an important tale of greed and propaganda, scientific corruption, and the bill coming due for our allowing a corporate elite to control and dictate our energy and environmental policies."

—John Stauber, founder of the Center for Media and Democracy

"Shearer pulls no punches in this extraordinary account of one Alaskan village's confrontation with the violence of climate change. Villagers sued fossil fuel companies for endangering their homeland and lying about it, underscoring the importance of sound science, traditional knowledge, and accurate information as critical ingredients for sustaining the climate justice movement. Shearer also considers the history of the "product defense industry," through which she links the politics of energy to a host of other sectors whose supporters have made it their business to manufacture doubt and misrepresentation about the risks associated with oil, coal, asbestos, lead, and tobacco. The casualties are adding up and they include public health, ecosystems, and our democracy. So where is the hope in all of this? It lies in the simple fact that the people of Kivalina fought back and struggled for a better world for themselves and for all of us."

—David Naguib Pellow, member of the board of directors of Greenpeace USA, author of *Resisting Global Toxics: Transnational Movements for Environmental Justice*, and Don Martindale Endowed Chair of Sociology at the University of Minnesota

"With *Kivalina: A Climate Change Story*, Christine Shearer has managed to do something quite remarkable, which is to take the incredibly complex geo/economic/political process of global climate change, present it in a way that is both comprehensible and compelling, and then directly link it to one of the first, bellwether communities to be affected by the process. The book is beautifully written and the community of Kivalina is a harbinger of what our failure to control our technology and our greed will be bringing to coastal communities and cities across the planet."

—Robert Gramling, coauthor of *Blowout in the Gulf: The BP Oil Spill Disaster and the Future of Energy in America* and professor of sociology at the University of Louisiana–Lafayette

"Kivalina, Shishmaref, Point Hope—three of the first communities, in this case all in the Arctic of Alaska, that are casualties of global climate change. Household names? No. But they should be. Christine Shearer, in *Kivalina: A Climate Change Story*, presents the human frustration and environmental evidence of devastation of one of these ancient Inupiat villages in a detailed and compelling fashion. Citing the tobacco and asbestos examples of "profit at all costs" corporate obfuscation, she makes the case that climate change is the latest on this sorry list of the failures of our corporations and their supporters in the federal and state governments to look past those profits to their dire consequences. Peter, Paul, and Mary, in their famous folk song, "Where Have All the Flowers Gone," can add another verse. Christine Shearer will write it."

—Harvard Ayers, senior author of *Arctic Gardens: Voices from an Abundant Land* and professor emeritus of anthropology at Appalachian State University

CONTENTS

ACKNOWLEDGMENTS

To Luke Cole, a strong advocate for environmental justice—your work lives on.

To William Freudenburg, an amazing mentor, professor, and friend whom I am lucky to have known.

To my grandparents, for all the years of love and encouragement, and for teaching me to stand up and fight for what I believe in, even when they disagreed with me.

To the lawyers, scholars, scientists, and government personnel who made time to speak with me.

To my family, friends, colleagues, and advisers for their help and encouragement. Big thanks to my parents, Iris and Rick, my brother Eric, my advisers John Foran, Lisa Hajjar, and Barbara Herr Harthorn, my informal adviser Richard Rood, and the UC Santa Barbara sociology graduate students for all their support.

Thank you to my CoalSwarm colleagues Ted Nace, Joshua Frank, and Bob Burton.

And to the people of Kivalina, who opened their homes to me.

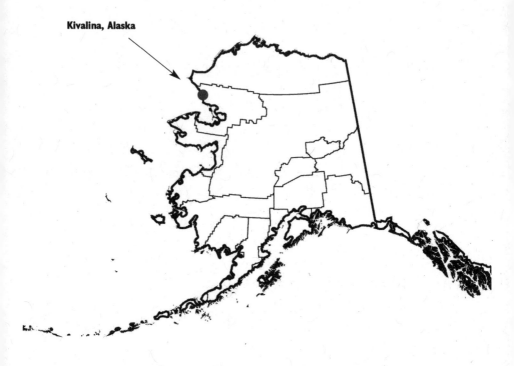

Kivalina, Alaska

FIELD NOTES FROM AUGUST 6, 2008

I flew to Anchorage, where the airport terminal is decorated in freeze-dried animals, and was picked up in a shuttle van from the hotel I'd booked. The driver asked why I was there in Alaska.

"Going to Kivalina."

"Why the hell you goin' there?"

"I'm interested in the lawsuit."

He laughed. "What a waste of time." He then told me that Al Gore was a "lying communist bastard," that the earth goes through changes—"Duh, girl, you heard of the Ice Age?"—and that it all really didn't matter anyway, because of the Rapture.

His voice was getting gruff and he abruptly pulled the van over. Mentally, I envisioned where I had put my pocketknife, when he suddenly pointed to a moose on the side of the road.

"Look at that," he said. "Beautiful, isn't it?"

I nodded. It was nighttime but still light out, and the moose stood tall next to some trees, barely noticing us.

He pulled forward and continued driving, and we moved from endless rows of green trees to downtown Anchorage, full of souvenir shops, hotels, and business buildings, one with the Chevron sign standing tall and prominent. The driver told me how he had drifted around different states since serving in the Vietnam War, and I suddenly felt bad for him; he has not had an easy life.

We got to the hotel, which was not exactly a Marriott, and a scruffy guy in hotel gear checked me in, then turned and started talking to a coworker about cocaine. It was still light outside when I fell asleep at 11 p.m.

I woke up at 4:30 a.m., the sun peeking out, to catch an early morning flight to Kotzebue, in the northwest part of the state. There I arrived at the tiniest airport I have ever been to, a one-room building where the baggage claim was a window from which luggage was periodically thrown out. As the room filled, I became acutely aware that I was the only person who did not know anyone else.

I walked across the airstrip to another small building to catch a cargo plane to Kivalina. The woman at the counter asked my weight. The boarding call was a guy yelling out, "Who's going to Kivalina?" I got up and followed him and a few others to a tiny plane. I checked the ground for parts, didn't see any, and climbed in.

There were seven of us onboard, and we seemed to make an unspoken agreement to sit on opposite sides so it did not tip over. The plane flew up noisily and wobbly. I looked out the window at long, curving watersheds, above the Arctic Circle and across the sea from Siberia.

Suddenly the plane began to descend, as if going into the sea. I looked out the pilot's front window and realized we were landing on a tiny, thin strip of land: Kivalina, surrounded on one side by the Chukchi Sea and the other by a lagoon. The north end was a small, dirt landing strip, and we looped around and down onto it.

I stepped off the plane, wondering what to do next, and was relieved when a woman on a small all-terrain vehicle asked, "Are you Christine?" I nodded and she introduced herself as Janet Mitchell, the city administrator whom I had spoken with briefly on the phone a few weeks earlier. I said hello and climbed on the back of her ATV, and she drove us south. Two minutes later we were already halfway down the island, and we pulled up in front of the city hall, a two-story wooden building.

Janet walked me toward the shoreline and told me Kivalina residents had been advised not to talk about the lawsuit. *Great*, I thought, wondering why I was there. But as Janet showed me the shrinking coastline and rapidly eroding bank, I realized the real issue for Kivalina is not necessarily the lawsuit. It is the relocation.

Kivalina was even smaller than I'd expected, despite having heard it was about two square miles and shrinking. Standing on the tiny island, only a few feet above sea level, we were completely surrounded by water. Janet walked me toward the Chukchi Sea. The western side of the island was a mess of bulldozers, trucks, and construction workers, working tirelessly to expand the shoreline, which was steadily eroding. The southern end was being armored with a seawall made of large rocks, and sandbags were spread about the ground.

Janet then walked me to the school, the largest building in Kivalina. The hallway was dark and cold. She introduced me to the school custodian, who noticed me shivering and laughed, saying the heat would be out all week, as I tried to hide my horror. They showed me to the teachers' lounge, my lodgings, and the locker room, my bathroom. Knowing many outside visitors seemingly cannot live without amenities such as indoor plumbing and a refrigerator, the city council had been sure to provide both, even though much of the village lived with neither. I felt both very pleased to have them and very spoiled and inept, a feeling that was not helped by my backpack being full of food, since I do not know how to hunt or fish like the villagers, who mainly live off the land.

Janet said goodbye and went back to work, while the school custodian and janitor sat in "my" new room, drinking coffee, looking at me with curiosity and smiling pleasantly. They made me some coffee and we talked for a bit, but I was feeling both slightly awkward and eager to explore. Excusing myself, I went out into the hallway. The school had a gymnasium and five or six classrooms, all of which were dark, as classes would not start for another few weeks.

I stepped outside and moved along the thin dirt road that circled the island, and then crossed through some homes toward the shoreline. With little plumbing in Kivalina, there were many "honey buckets" buried in the ground and used as restrooms. Homes were decorated with caribou antlers, and caribou skins hung from wire like drying laundry. I walked toward the lagoon, which circled the eastern end of Kivalina and poured into the sea, cutting off the village from nearby bodies of land. The lagoon was also eating away at the island, and a small home was beginning to have its base eroded, hanging over the coastline. I pulled out my camera to take pictures, while large mosquitoes buzzed around my face and launched at me like little bombers, biting me through my sweater. I sprayed myself with repellent, remembering the travel agent telling me, only half-joking, that mosquitoes were the Alaska state bird. A nearby resident looked at me as I took pictures, swatted at the air, and sprayed myself, and I realized I was not doing a very good job at blending in.

I got back on the main road and moved toward the northern end of the island, toward the airstrip. As I walked, a group of little kids ran up to me, yelling "Teacher! Teacher!" since each school year new teachers come to the island. I told them I was not a teacher, but whoever I was mattered little to them, and they took my hand and said they would walk with me, singing songs and showing me their toys. One of the kids grabbed my camera and started running, and I chased after him yelling, "Please don't break it!" while he laughed. He finally handed it back to me, after accidentally dropping it, then ran up the side of a huge pile of dirt. Other kids followed, so I followed, and we ran up and down the dirt mound like it was a mini rollercoaster. As we played on the mound overlooking Kivalina, I tried not to think about how that dirt was probably being used for beach nourishment, and that these kids were in danger, playing blissfully in a construction zone on an island that is disappearing.

INTRODUCTION

In February 2008, a tiny Alaska Native village named Kivalina filed suit against twenty-four fossil fuel companies for contributing to the village's erosion through large amounts of greenhouse gas emissions, and for creating a false debate around climate change. The lawsuit was filed in conjunction with environmental justice and indigenous rights organizations as one of several steps in a broader push for climate justice, aiming to help Kivalina residents draw attention to their situation and call for action from government and corporate officials that had so far largely ignored them.

The media gave the lawsuit brief attention that quickly faded, and the judge's ruling was issued with little discussion or notice outside of certain legal circles. Meanwhile, the people of Kivalina are still in danger from the effects of climate change, in a situation that is going to become more common throughout the world.

For roughly the past ten thousand years we have enjoyed a relatively stable climate that has allowed for the development of agriculture and civilization. Such stability is the exception, not the norm, when it comes to the earth's 4.54-billion-year history. The earth has oscillated between long periods of cooling (glaciations) and shorter periods of warming (interglacials), sometimes undergoing radical climate variations within the span of a century or even a decade. Evidence suggests that later glaciations correspond with periodic shifts in the earth's orbit, tilt, and precession (movement of the axis), which can reduce the amount of energy received at the poles. This small temperature disturbance, in turn, can kick-start a glaciation through feedbacks: as ice builds, greenhouse concentrations are sequestered within the oceans and reduced in the atmosphere, and the ice reflects a greater amount of sunlight back to space (the "albedo effect"). These processes maintain the cooling and can create the conditions for layer upon layer of cumulative ice sheets.[1]

Glaciations then give way to warmer interglacial periods, which have been correlated to increases in greenhouse gases in the atmosphere—trace gases, such as carbon dioxide and methane, that capture heat and can amplify the effects of orbital shifts. The sun's light rays that are absorbed by oceans, land, and vegetation are eventually released as infrared radiation, or heat energy. Due to their molecular structure (three or more atoms), greenhouse gases vibrate at frequencies that allow them to absorb and emit this infrared radiation, sending a portion of the energy back to the earth's surface. During certain periods this increased heat can hasten the melting of glaciers; the newly exposed landscape then absorbs more heat and releases more greenhouse gases, potentially leading to an interglacial period.[2] The most recent warming shift occurred 11,700 years ago, the beginning of a relatively long and mild interglacial period known as the Holocene, in which we are presently living.

Some have argued, however, that the Holocene epoch has been supplanted by an Anthropocene epoch, or human-influenced climate, beginning with large-scale agriculture and accelerating rapidly with the Industrial Revolution and the widespread use of fossil fuels. For the past two centuries we have been digging up and burning fossilized carbon from earlier eras—coal, oil, and natural gas—at an accelerating rate, and greatly increasing the amount of greenhouse gases in our atmosphere. While we need greenhouse gases to absorb heat and sustain life on earth, their increasing concentration is steadily turning up the furnace on our lower atmosphere and altering our climate. Scientists are concerned not only because the effects are already apparent in the form of events such as melting glaciers, rising sea levels, and increased water vapor in the atmosphere, but also because the ultimate consequences are so disturbing. Historic evidence suggests the earth has certain feedback mechanisms that can tip the planet toward extreme cooling as well as extreme heating—and reversing those mechanisms can be very difficult, if not impossible, once they hit a certain threshold.[3]

As of 2011, carbon dioxide levels are about 390 parts per million (ppm), substantially higher and more rapidly built up than at any time in the eight hundred thousand years' worth of records from air bubbles trapped in ice cores. Numerous glaciers are melting faster than many had predicted,[4] and the thawing permafrost—the frozen subsoil beneath the ice—can release stores of carbon dioxide as well as methane, with a high and rapid heat absorption much stronger than that of carbon dioxide. The most pressing question is what large amounts of greenhouse gases will do to an already warm interglacial period. Some scientists predict that events such as the melting of glaciers and the resulting steady release of methane could bring about a "tipping point," setting off a cascade of warming feedbacks over which we would no longer have any control. Other scientists believe we are already at or very near that tipping point, and need to clamp down on greenhouse gas emissions immediately.[5]

Despite these vocal concerns, pockets of the U.S. population remain unconvinced of the existence of human-caused (anthropogenic) warming, its potential severity, and the need for action. This includes people who believe climate change is a hoax; fossil fuel company executives reluctant to alter their business practices; members of think tanks, the media, and other organizations that are actively trying to distort the science on climate change; and representatives of the U.S. federal government, particularly the George W. Bush administration and certain members of Congress, who have been complicit in downplaying the reality and severity of climate change.

Meanwhile, some are already feeling the daily effects of global warming. Among them are Alaska Natives living in the now steadily melting Arctic, such as the residents of Kivalina. Sea ice no longer adequately forms on Kivalina's coastline, leaving the tiny island—perched on a thin strip of land between a sea and a lagoon—vulnerable to storms and erosion, and requiring relocation. Amid government inaction on climate change, the village filed suit against fossil fuel companies for their relocation costs, estimated at $100–$400 million, and for creating a false debate around global warming: *Kivalina v. ExxonMobil et al.*

In taking a close look at the political, cultural, and economic dynamics surrounding the Kivalina lawsuit, this book will detail the development of the product defense industry (PDI), an entire business area designed to help large industries stave off regulations and laws. It will then explore how the PDI, fused with the fossil fuel industry's strong and innate position within the U.S. and world economy, has helped prevent U.S. action on climate change. The result is a political environment in which it has been incredibly difficult to adequately address what is increasingly a clear and present danger, particularly for those already affected, such as the residents of Kivalina. While individuals can scale back on the amount and type of energy they consume, the impact of such actions is limited without broader societal change. How to initiate effective action? People around the world are working on the answers right now. And for the village of Kivalina, the clock is ticking.

AFTER A TWO-NIGHT BATTLE with the Chukchi Sea, the message was clear: the village of Kivalina must be moved. Adapting to our environment was no longer possible. The only option left for the Inupiaq people of Kivalina was to get out of the way and let the impacts of climate change take their toll on the small barrier island. According to the Army Corps of Engineers, after a rock revetment is built to keep the island together, the village has ten to fifteen years to continue to inhabit the island. That is the amount of time that the rock revetment, begun in 2008, has bought for Kivalina. But it does not address the potential of flooding due to the rising sea level. The land failure that occurred after the 2004 storm also had an unexpected outcome: climate change is melting the coastline. Where will we go, and who will help us move?

—KIVALINA TRIBAL ADMINISTRATOR COLLEEN SWAN

ONE

BLUEPRINT FOR DENIAL

You often think about the way history works as kind of a set of unintended consequences, consequences of well-meaning people that basically are trying their best in a number of ways to deal with a problem as they see it and within a special historical moment, to have special historical context. You kind of avoid the idea that there are conspiracies or that there are people planning the world in a certain way. You just try to avoid that because it's— it seems too—too unreal and too frightening in its implications. Yet, when you look at these documents, you say "Yes, there are people who understood what was going on, people who thought about the crisis that was engulfing them or about to engulf them and tried in every which way to get out of that crisis and to actually shape public opinion, shape professional opinion, and also shape government's opinion about an issue that was really dangerous."
  —Public health historian David Rosner, *Trade Secrets*

Your people say global warming is not happening because they don't live our lives, or see our snow, our ice, how it's melting.
  —Kivalina resident David Frankson, August 8, 2008

It would be hard to exaggerate Kivalina's precarious position. The tiny village sits on a thin strip of land, a quarter mile across at its widest point, and is sandwiched between the Chukchi Sea and Kivalina

Aerial view of Kivalina, 2008

Lagoon, at the mouths of the Wulik and Kivalina Rivers. The sea's waves eat at the shore from the west and the water slowly undercuts it from the east. The worst threats, however, come from the storms, which have swallowed as much as seventy feet in one downpour. Kivalina traditionally enjoyed protection from storms by sea ice formation, which surrounded and hardened the coastline. For the past three decades, however, the ice has formed later in the year and melted earlier, leaving the shore vulnerable to quick and dangerous erosion from storms. With a maximum elevation of only ten feet above sea level, Kivalina residents have lived on constant alert.

Since the storms of 2004, the village has lost about a hundred feet of coastline from erosion, in some areas exposing the permafrost and further destabilizing the shore. A protective seawall literally washed away in 2006, and in 2007 another devastating storm prompted an evacuation of the village. Climate change was coming more quickly and severely, putting the entire community in danger.

Meanwhile, halfway around the world, "Climategate" erupted. In November 2009, the emails, documents, and source code of Climatic Research Unit (CRU) scientists at the University of East Anglia were hacked and publicized, and soon various news organizations declared the information cast serious doubt on the validity of climate change science. FoxNews.com's John Lott wrote, "A coordinated campaign to hide scientific information about climate change appears unprecedented. Could it wind up costing us *trillions*?" (November 24, 2009, emphasis his), while a *Wall Street Journal* op-ed of December 8, 2009, read, "The tip of the Climategate iceberg: The global warming scandal is bigger than one e-mail leak."

As the smoke cleared, however, investigations by the Associated Press,[1] the House of Commons, and the independent Science Assessment Panel, among others, found most of the CRU scientists' emails actually expressed frustration at being harassed by climate change skeptics, exasperation over research conducted by nonscientists in conjunction with fossil fuel industry think tanks, and difficulties with some particularities of data—a far cry from undercutting the scientific consensus on climate change. In short, most of the emails said more about the actions of climate change "skeptics" than about the validity of climate change science. Further, questions were rarely raised regarding who hacked the CRU server and emails and why. How did these emails become widely translated into news stories declaring global warming a hoax—stories that persist to this day?

Climategate is emblematic of the "discourse of doubt" deliberately employed by the fossil fuel industry and its allies. This discourse sets up certainty as the only acceptable standard for acknowledging and thus acting on climate change, while simultaneously manufacturing uncertainty, to ensure such certainty is never achieved.[2] Demanding certainty is also a deliberate misrepresentation of science, as science consists of gathering and assessing reliable data, producing replicable results, establishing areas of consensus, and building on the findings for greater understanding, while acknowledging areas in need of further research.[3] In demanding certainty while manufacturing uncertainty, industries can forever frame the discussion as "the science is out and more research is needed," delaying regulations indefinitely even when evidence of harm and danger is overwhelming.

With the slickly executed and damaging Climategate, the fossil fuel industry and its allies applied a twenty-first-century upgrade to a well-established blueprint and organizational structure for manufacturing uncertainty, developed in previous decades by other industries, namely asbestos, lead, and tobacco. These three were among the first manufacturers whose products were later found to be harmful. Generating doubt did not begin as a conscious tactic of these industries but developed as they became increasingly unable to control scientific research, suppress negative findings, and stave off government regulations. These efforts grew into what assistant secretary of labor for Occupational Safety and Health (OSHA) David Michaels has called the "product defense industry," or PDI.[4] The PDI is made up of lawyers, public relations firms, think tanks, and sophisticated, specialized organizations that go beyond traditional PR duties to undertake the shaping of not just public opinion but also scientific research, government regulation, and legal opinion. PDI organizations tend to portray environmental and health risks as minimal or nonexistent, and as secondary to the supposed economic costs of regulation, which are portrayed as inevitably dire, not just for a given corporation but also for U.S. consumers and the economy as a whole. The PDI's goal is to delay and avoid government regulation, regardless of the costs to the public.

CORPORATIONS, REGULATION, AND SCIENCE

Corporations were originally regulated by states and granted existence via state charters that included stipulations such as public access to records, shareholder liability, limited duration, and restrictions on geographic reach and stock ownership in other companies. In the mid-1800s, however, businesses began convincing state legislatures to loosen restrictions, helping industries to branch out into other states while continuing to enjoy the more lenient standards of the "home" state. States that relaxed standards saw higher revenues, leading other states to do likewise as well as to offer concessions to attract industry. By the late 1800s, the state charter system had been largely undone, and corporations were granted approval with few of the previous restrictions. This allowed for the growth of large, national corporations with big profits and political influence—and strong incentives to stay in business and stave off public regulation. Their growing size also led to increasing layers of management and decreasing levels of individual contact and responsibility between corporate decision makers and the people they served.

As corporations grew, the federal government was reluctant to rein in their power, even granting land and subsidies to modern industries such as railroads and coal under the rationale that to support industry was to uphold the national values of economic growth and industrial development. The reluctance to regulate increased after World Wars I and II, the first global-scale wars fought with modern industrial technology—petroleum, tanks, aircraft, chemicals, and related weaponry. Wartime needs prompted massive government investment in the expansion of these business sectors, which then paved the way for the post–World War II consumer boom.

Due to the delayed onset of negative effects (also known as "latency period") of many hazardous and toxic materials, by the time strong evidence of their risks had accumulated, many of the profiting industries had grown large and influential, with powerful allies in the U.S. government.[5] Anyone who sought to mitigate the risks had little institutional framework in which to do so: before the 1960s there were few regulatory bodies, and they had limited enforcement powers and finances. Studies of perceived public risks were therefore often funded by or in cooperation with the industries involved. An early example is asbestos.

ASBESTOS

Asbestos is a form of magnesium silicate, made up of microscopic, chainlike fibers so light they can float for days.[6] Since the fibers are tiny and yet made of rock they are extremely flexible, strong, and resistant to heat and water. They can be braided into strands or mixed into products

such as cement, making asbestos popular for fireproofing, electrical insulation, building materials, brake linings, and chemical filters. Asbestos
use grew with the manufacturing needs of World Wars I and II. Unfortunately, small asbestos fibers can flake off into the environment and are
easily inhaled, lodging in the lungs or other organs and accumulating
for years or decades until manifesting as disease.

By the late 1920s, the term "asbestosis" was being used in medical
literature to refer to an inflammatory lung disease that caused irreversible scarring of the lung tissue. At the time, however, reports of asbestosis were overshadowed by the widespread attention paid to silica
dust, a hard mineral used in glass and cement, as a result of the Hawks
Nest disaster of 1927. The disaster led to the deaths of an estimated
seven hundred workers, many of them Black migrant workers from the
South, who were deliberately diverted by Union Carbide to drill
through the most silica-rich areas of a mountain without protective
masks, despite reports from workers and medical professionals that inhalation of silica particles leads to serious, debilitating respiratory problems,[7] a condition known as silicosis. Pressure from the labor movement
brought the disaster to congressional hearings and public attention.

In response to Hawks Nest and public concerns over safety, companies involved in the "dusty industries" formed the Air Hygiene Foundation, later known as the Industrial Hygiene Foundation, to plan a public
relations campaign and offer an "undistorted picture" of the subject.[8] The
foundation recruited leading scientists and public officials to serve as
members and trustees, establishing itself as a major resource for occupational lung disease research. Among its stated purposes was to limit corporate liability by placing silica, asbestos, and coal dust exposure in
workers' compensation schemes, an approach that also had the effect of
removing workers' right to sue the company over these kinds of exposure.[9]

By the late 1930s, the Air Hygiene Foundation had 225 member companies and established research links with Harvard University and the Mellon Institute.[10] The foundation encouraged member industries to begin limiting the worst abuses of exposure through precautionary measures such as masks, wetted dust, and improved ventilation. These technological initiatives were then used by the Air Hygiene Foundation as the basis for determining industry standards of acceptable dust exposure for workers. In 1936, the foundation was invited by the U.S. Department of Labor to a conference on silicosis, and its standard for silica exposure was subsequently adopted by the U.S. Public Health Service as a voluntary safety threshold.[11] As stated by public health historians Gerald Markowitz and David Rosner, "We now think of thresholds as being the result of scientific study and analysis, but…the standard for silica was established retrospectively and as part of a political compromise that traded on workers' health."[12] Markowitz also explained that industry scientists "understood that if they set a figure of X as a threshold limit value, it didn't represent safety, and yet that is how it was presented to the workforce."[13]

The same voluntary standard was then applied to asbestos. When some scientists disagreed with the standard, saying it lacked demonstrable proof in preventing disease and was based upon technological feasibility rather than science, legal counsel to the asbestos industry turned the argument on its head. They suggested that since there was no *demonstrably safe* level, the threshold determined from their data would have to suffice in the face of scientific uncertainty—despite limited studies being undertaken by the industry to address and lessen that uncertainty.[14]

Turning the potential dangers of industrial dusts into a scientific debate over acceptable threshold levels not only assuaged public fears but also had the effect of taking the public out of the discussion, making industrial risks such as asbestos a matter for "experts." This allowed industries to claim authority over the subject and to recruit researchers and doctors conducting studies in the area, who had few alternative sources of research funding at the time. Through the 1920s and '30s, the asbestos industry agreed to finance experiments on asbestos dust, as long as companies maintained control over disclosure of the results.[15] They hoped the studies would show asbestos was not dangerous. Many studies, however, showed that asbestos was not only as bad as silica, but actually much worse, with asbestosis affecting both workers and miners regardless of workplace adherence to threshold levels.[16] Rather than publicizing the studies and warning workers, the industry suppressed the results and instead argued that asbestosis was not a serious disease, and was due to poor factory conditions or excessive smoking by workers, not to the asbestos fiber itself.[17]

In the 1940s and '50s, inhalation studies began linking asbestos to cancer, and industry efforts at suppression were dealt a serious blow when a 1964 conference was organized around asbestos and its harmful effects, particularly its link to the painful and fatal cancer mesothelioma.[18] In 1966, the first asbestos product lawsuit was filed by Claude Tomplait, a worker diagnosed with asbestosis; one year later, the asbestos manufacturer Johns Manville hired the public relations firm Hill & Knowlton. The firm was formed in 1927 by John Hill, a former employee of the steel industry who disliked organized labor and felt that the public debate was one-sided and biased against corporations, an attitude that only heightened as the role of government alongside industry expanded through the New Deal. Rather than merely presenting the corporate side of a debate, however, over time Hill & Knowlton became involved in false advertising, political bribery, and coercing or paying journalists for favorable media coverage of their clients.[19] For asbestos, Hill & Knowlton advised the industry to admit to the hazards of asbestos "where they are demonstrable," and created the Asbestos Information Association to refute scientific studies implicating asbestos as harmful.[20]

Workers facing debilitating lung problems and cancer, however, knew of the harms. As disabled and ill workers fought to have their medical expenses paid, many asbestos manufacturers slowly started moving toward alternative materials through the 1970s and '80s. Public health historian Barry Castleman believes this shift marked the true decline of U.S. asbestos manufacturers: "The companies found it was easier to start using alternative materials than face liability. That's what really started bringing the industry down."[21]

As part of a wave of 1970s federal regulations, in 1971 OSHA issued the first asbestos-exposure standard. In 1975 asbestos insulation products were banned in the United States, although asbestos can still be found in old buildings across the country, as was evidenced by the manifestation of asbestos-related diseases following the September 11, 2001, collapse of the World Trade Center in New York. When the Environmental Protection Agency (EPA) tried to ban asbestos altogether in 1989, however, it was prohibited by a federal court of appeals. The court found that the EPA, despite a decade of research on the health risks of asbestos, had "presented insufficient evidence" and thus failed to meet the legal requirements of the Toxic Substances Control Act.[22] No other uses or imports of asbestos have been banned since 1991, and products containing asbestos continue to be manufactured and imported, such as a denser form of asbestos-containing cement used in pipes, sheets, and shingles. Due to concerted efforts by segments of the asbestos industry, worldwide asbestos production actually rebounded after 2000, and is now at levels roughly equivalent to those of the 1960s, before the widespread awareness of harm.[23]

The asbestos case demonstrates the early influence industries wielded over the scope of research and dissemination of results, and thus over public understanding of what constitutes risk. Regulations were shaped in accordance with economic and technological concerns rather than scientific ones, with definitive proof established as the only acceptable standard for stronger regulations. Harmful findings were systematically suppressed, disputed, and denied, with the industry turning to public relations to rebrand its product as safe in the public eye and stave off regulation. The same early influence of corporate economic concerns over science and public health, and the use of certainty as the only acceptable threshold for regulation, can also be seen with lead.

LEAD

Lead is a malleable metal that has been used for thousands of years because it is widespread and easy to work with. It was found in the water pipes of the Roman Empire; the word "plumbing" stems from the Latin root for lead, *plumbum*. Unfortunately, lead is also a neurotoxin that accumulates in soft tissues and bones, damaging nerve connections and leading to brain and blood disorders.

Public health historians have traced scientific research on the dangers of lead poisoning to the nineteenth century and clinical descriptions to centuries earlier. In the 1920s, exposure to lead paint was tied to learning disabilities. In 1922, League of Nations members signed an agreement forbidding the use of white-lead interior paint. The United States did not join in the prohibition, even though many U.S. specialists believed that lead paint posed a hazard.[24]

By the 1930s, health specialists were sufficiently alarmed about lead paint to advise that it be replaced with safer alternatives, such as titanium- and zinc-based paints. Rather than transitioning to alternatives, however, the National Lead Company (now known as NL Industries) and other white-lead producers formed the trade group Lead Industries Association (LIA) to promote the increased use of lead paint. LIA formed alliances in academia, most notably with Harvard researcher Dr. Joseph Aub, who claimed that eating lead paint did not harm children; rather, he argued, to eat the paint they must have already been "defective" due to other factors, such as nutritional deficiencies and poverty.[25] The National Lead Company sought to assuage parental concerns about lead's effects on children through the Dutch Boy advertisements, featuring a child carrying a paint brush and bucket, and even created a coloring book for children entitled *The Dutch Boy's Lead Party*. The industry also ratcheted up production, launching the White Lead Promotion campaign in 1938 to encourage the use of lead paint in urban and public housing, and convincing schools, hotels, and even health departments to use their product, in an attempt to associate lead with whiteness and sanitation in the public mind.[26]

In 1943, *Time* magazine published an article about the relationship between lead exposure and learning disabilities in children. In response, lead paint manufacturers hired Hill & Knowlton—the same PR firm employed later by the asbestos industry—to counteract the medical and public "misinformation" and resist local efforts at regulation. Hill & Knowlton first produced a report on childhood lead poisoning, *then* searched for a scientist to act as the author.[27] As the use of alternatives to lead grew, in 1955 the paint industry issued a voluntary standard limiting the amount of lead in interior paint.[28] Communities, especially those with public housing in which lead paint had been heavily used and promoted, pushed for a full, mandatory ban on lead paint and its removal from housing. LIA responded by maintaining that lead was dangerous only at high levels, and lead poisoning was a result of irresponsible parenting.[29]

Lead manufacturers also defended the use of lead in gasoline, as adding lead raises engine compression and speed, preventing engine "knock." The industry argued that this product, tetraethyl lead, did not have the toxic characteristics of lead itself, and dissolved harmlessly into the atmosphere. Lead was therefore added to gasoline for decades.[30] In the 1960s, geochemist Clair Patterson documented a correlation between the industrial use of lead and its increasing presence in ice core drillings in Greenland. This increase could also be seen in U.S. residents, whose lead levels were shown to be significantly higher than those found in prehistoric bones.[31] Patterson's research showed what many public health advocates had long asserted: lead does not just dissipate or disappear. It accumulates—in the atmosphere, in neighborhoods, and in peoples' bodies. Herbert Needleman, a pediatrician who had worked for DuPont and noted the glazed look of workers involved with tetraethyl fabrication, went on to show that even at low levels in the body lead is harmful, associated with lower IQs and shorter attention spans.[32] Unable to stave off the public backlash, lead was gradually phased out of gasoline beginning in the 1970s and banned from paint in 1978, despite industry efforts and objections.

The lead industry responded to growing scientific evidence of public harm by creating doubt, while marketing its products directly to children and increasing production. Children still suffer from lead poisoning, many of them in areas with older housing where lead paint was insufficiently or never removed.[33] Lead can also still be found in soil and food. Meanwhile, actions to suppress and discredit scientific research were taken to new levels by the tobacco industry, which turned the manufacturing of scientific doubt into an industry of its own, helping to launch an increasingly sophisticated product defense industry (PDI).

TOBACCO

When asked how tobacco differed from the lead and asbestos industries in terms of public relations and science, OSHA official and public health historian David Michaels said, "It was tobacco that really turned product defense into an art."[34] By the early 1900s, several tobacco manufacturers had already established themselves as multimillion-dollar companies. At the time, little was known about the health effects of smoking, as there was only circumstantial evidence. The prevailing sense was that while smoking was probably harmful, the effects were not dire, as summed up by a 1936 article in *Scientific American*: "Most smokers...are doubtless harmed to some extent, usually not great, by smoking."[35] There were reports, however, that incidences of lung cancer were on the rise, and in 1938 the first scientific study linking lung cancer to smoking was published.[36] By the mid-1950s, multiple studies associating cigarette smoking with disease had been completed.[37]

As worries about the risks of smoking grew and cigarette sales dropped, tobacco companies hired none other than Hill & Knowlton to handle the industry's public relations campaign. To counter the growing health concerns, in 1954 Hill & Knowlton set up the Tobacco Industry Research Committee (later the Center for Tobacco Research), which advised the companies to market filtered cigarettes and "low-tar" formulations that promised a "healthier" smoke. That same year Hill & Knowlton also oversaw the release of "A Frank Statement to Cigarette Smokers," a full-page editorial-advertisement run in newspapers throughout the United States, which questioned scientific

reports on smoking and announced the formation of a scientific committee to conduct research and assuage public concerns.[38] The public
responded to the ad and the "healthier" tobacco options, with sales remaining steady. Later, "low-tar" and filtered cigarettes were found to
be no safer than regular cigarettes.[39]

By the late 1950s, however, several states had proposed tobacco regulations. To defeat such legislation, in 1958 fourteen major cigarette producers formed the Tobacco Institute, hoping to put a positive spin on the
industry. Meanwhile, tobacco companies continued to fund the Center
for Tobacco Research, officially announcing that they wanted to see if
cigarette smoke could be made "safer" while still delivering nicotine.[40]

In 1964, the surgeon general released a landmark report that
stated, "Cigarette smoking is a health hazard of sufficient importance
in the United States to warrant appropriate remedial action."[41] At
House and Senate committee hearings on the report, the tobacco industry presented a number of its physicians, who testified that they
disagreed with the findings and that there was "no proof" that cigarette
smoking was harmful, deliberately ignoring that while there was not
definitive proof, there was substantial evidence.[42] In 1965, under the
Cigarette Labeling and Advertising Act, cigarette makers agreed to
put warning labels on their products, encouraged by legal counsel who
suggested the labels could act as a buffer against strict liability. Heavy
lobbying by the industry softened the language on the warning labels
to read that smoking "may" be harmful. Indeed, the warning labels in
some ways aided the industry, as it could be claimed in lawsuits that
smokers had been forewarned.[43] In 1969, Congress banned the broadcast advertising of tobacco.

Although both statutes were weaker than those originally proposed, the industry was on edge. It was becoming evident that a "safe

cigarette" was not achievable or even desirable, since marketing such a product could be tantamount to admitting the industry knew cigarettes were harmful. Advised by its lawyers that any admission of harm could open the floodgates of litigation, the tobacco industry directed its research efforts toward studies that questioned the link between tobacco and disease. The strategy was later summed up by an internal tobacco memo: "Doubt is our product."[44] In 1966, the Center for Tobacco Research began to fund "special projects" decided not by the industry's scientists, but by its lawyers,[45] and based primarily on legal concerns: studies questioning or refuting the link between tobacco smoke and disease could be presented as evidence in a trial. Scientific research was passed through industry lawyers so that it could be marked "confidential" and thus enjoy attorney-client privilege in litigation.[46] Hill & Knowlton objected to these special projects, either because the process was ethically questionable or because it was taking away from the PR firm's control, or both. In any case, Hill & Knowlton resigned.

By the 1980s, cigarette makers had a new issue to contend with: environmental tobacco smoke, also called secondhand smoke. Evidence of the health risks of secondhand smoke was mounting quickly, with 28 articles published by 1981 and 213 articles by 1989.[47] In 1992, the EPA reported that secondhand smoke was a human lung carcinogen, causally associated with an increased risk of respiratory infections in children, and began moving toward its regulation. The Tobacco Institute, the coalition of major producers, immediately dismissed the EPA report as a triumph of "political correctness over sound science," and paid a group of scientists thousands of dollars to write letters to influential scientific journals disputing the EPA report, including the *Journal of the American Medical Association*.[48]

Despite all its efforts, by 1994 the tobacco industry could not stave off the overwhelming evidence. An ABC broadcast claimed tobacco companies had been spiking their cigarettes with extra nicotine to hook smokers, leading to a Senate hearing on tobacco industry practices in which CEOs testified under oath that nicotine was not addictive and cigarettes did not cause disease. Then internal documents from the cigarette manufacturer Brown & Williamson were leaked to the public, revealing the tobacco company had known about but withheld research findings on the highly addictive nature of nicotine and the harmful effects of cigarette smoke.[49] States sued to recoup medical costs for smoking-related illnesses, leading to the release of more industry documents.

Internal documents showed the tobacco industry was not just working to protect its own industry, but also linking up with other industries to affect the national consciousness about science and risk.[50] Documents of cigarette manufacturing giant Philip Morris detailed how, as the EPA moved to regulate secondhand smoke, Philip Morris hired public relations firm APCO Worldwide, created by legal counsel Arnold & Porter, which advised the cigarette manufacturer to set up a national coalition to educate the media, the public, and public officials on the dangers of "junk science."[51] This coalition became known as The Advancement of Sound Science Coalition (TASSC). To give TASSC the appearance of being a grassroots citizens' organization, APCO advised that TASSC have a broad group of contributors and issues, both for credibility and liability purposes: if Philip Morris were asked at trial if TASSC were a tobacco front group, they could say no. TASSC created the website www.junkscience.com, which offered a platform for attacks against government-funded science and regulation. It was run by a columnist for the website of Fox News, Steve Milloy, who had previously worked for APCO. Shortly after TASSC was founded, many industry representatives and even political officials started employing the terms "junk" and "sound" science.[52] Internal documents also revealed that tobacco officials were hiring companies and consultants to fight against stronger epidemiological standards in the regulation of secondhand smoke, such as the Harvard Center for Risk Analysis, which argued in its publications that EPA research on secondhand smoke was not based on sound science.[53]

PDI TACTICS WITHIN THE U.S. GOVERNMENT

While large segments of the U.S. population fought in the 1960s and '70s for civil and social rights and the institutionalization of workplace, consumer safety, and environmental regulations, a "New Right" countermovement began forming in the 1970s seeking to infuse industry tactics regarding science and regulation into government policy. Although pushing for neoliberalism, or the separation of government from the market, many New Right efforts would more accurately be described as increasing corporate influence over government. Conservative businessmen such as Joseph Coors and billionaire Richard Mellon Scaife created large foundations that funded a new wave of neoliberal think tanks conflating corporate freedom with individual freedom. Coors, notably, also created the Coalition on Revival, a network of evangelical leaders devoted to the idea that a theocratic type of government must be created before Jesus will return,[54] illustrating the budding confluence between neoliberals opposed to regulation and fundamentalist Christians who regard much of science and government policy as incongruous with the Bible.[55]

The efforts of the New Right helped secure the presidency of Ronald Reagan. Reagan, in turn, moved toward dismantling regulatory reforms by staffing agencies with industry representatives who had been vocal and active in their opposition to the very agencies they were now appointed to head. Coors associate Anne Gorsuch was put in charge of the EPA, cattle baron Robert Burford was made head of the Bureau of Land Management, and natural resources secretary of the U.S. Chamber of Commerce James Watt was appointed head of the Department of Interior. The new appointees promptly slashed budgets and staffs and reduced government enforcement, leaving these new agencies vulnerable—intentionally, it seems—to being captured and dismantled by industry interests.[56] The Reagan administration also adopted the strategy of doubt, echoing the National Coal Association as it called for more research on acid rain before the implementation of any regulations on sulfur dioxide emissions from coal plants.[57] The administration also repealed the Fairness Doctrine in 1987, which had been designed to promote "honest, equitable, and balanced" news.[58]

Additionally, Reagan strengthened the Office of Information and Regulatory Affairs (OIRA), created in 1980 and headed by Jim Tozzi before he became a consultant for the tobacco industry. OIRA requires all pending government regulations to pass through it for cost-benefit analysis before implementation, adding another bureaucratic layer in which regulations can be reinterpreted and whittled down.[59] Throughout its history, OIRA has helped replace scientific standards for regulation with economic ones, determined by a small executive panel whose deliberations and records are largely inaccessible to the public.[60] OIRA can therefore not only reinterpret regulations, but also do so with little public accountability.

While Reagan helped facilitate the industry capture of government agencies and regulations, the Gingrich Congress helped facilitate the industry capture of government-funded science. Shortly after the new Republican majority took power over Congress in 1995, they dismantled the process in place for evaluating scientific and technical data by abolishing the Congressional Office of Technology Assessment, a bipartisan agency created in 1972 that analyzed scientific and technological data to help government officials make informed evaluations. Without the agency, government representatives are free to regard science as a marketplace of ideas—and to give equal or more weight to paid industry contrarians than to peer-reviewed scientific studies, as seen with the 1995 congressional hearing questioning ozone depletion long after the issue had been settled within the scientific community.[61] By calling into question established scientific fact, conservative contrarians portray themselves as modern-day Galileos, defending marginalized ideas against mainstream scientific dogma, an idea epitomized in the book *Galileo's Revenge* by Peter Huber of the Manhattan Institute, a conservative think tank.

To challenge government-funded science further, Congress passed the Shelby Amendment in 1998, making government research available under Freedom of Information Act requests, as well as the Data Quality Act (DQA), allowing for the filing of legal claims against the dissemination of government research. Both pieces of legislation allowed industry to gain access to and thus challenge government research at its earliest stages, and were drafted by Phillip Morris consultant Jim Tozzi. Corporate-funded research, meanwhile, is not subject to the same open-access requirements.

While downplaying and attacking government science, those opposed to regulations have also drummed up support by funding research institutes, such as the Harvard Center for Risk Analysis, that produce primarily dire economic analyses of the possible consequences of regulation. Such reports have contributed to a widespread public perception that regulation in any form is inevitably expensive, an assumption even Democratic officials rarely question.[62] These analyses seldom factor in, however, the costs already borne by society due to increased sickness and disease and thus medical care, as well as environmental degradation and cleanup—public costs that therefore act as invisible subsidies to industry. Such cost-benefit analyses also systematically downplay or ignore the value and benefits of a healthy society and healthy ecosystems.[63]

PDI research and cost-benefit analyses are then publicized by conservative think tanks, whose large budgets allow them disproportionate attention in the media,[64] giving them public access greater than the strength of their research. Repeal of the Fairness Doctrine has further enabled the growth of media networks such as Fox that publicize and amplify PDI views. These tactics have created an artificial, "postmodern" reality of multiple "scientific" opinions, ignoring crucial factors such as reliability of research and clusters of scientific consensus.

Perhaps the most chilling effect of industry and government actions has been the nurturing of widespread, dogmatic skepticism among sections of the general public,[65] leading to clusters of the U.S. population that are unconvinced of harm or danger, regardless of the weight of scientific evidence. Many people have also been persuaded to give up their rights to hold corporations accountable, not just through regulations, but in the court of law, as discussed in the next chapter.

KIVALINA IS A SMALL INUPIAQ village in Northwest Arctic Alaska that sits on a barrier reef island. The village sits there because, in 1905, the Bureau of Indian Affairs came and built a school on the island, informing the people who lived in the geographic area that they had to bring their children to the school to be educated or face imprisonment. Historically the island had only been used for seasonal hunting and fishing. The Inupiaq people complied and brought their children to the school from their individual settlements on the outskirts of the barrier island, an area that was and still is their aboriginal territory.

Over time, life became difficult and the parents were concerned that they were endangering the lives of their children by bringing them to and from school during winter storms and subzero temperatures. "Winter" constitutes approximately nine months out of the year in this part of the world. The parents began moving their families to the island permanently, and that began a different life for them in what is now a village called Kivalina.

—KIVALINA TRIBAL ADMINISTRATOR COLLEEN SWAN

TWO

SHAPING LEGALITY

In January 2010, the U.S. Supreme Court ruled in *Citizens United v. Federal Election Commission* that a campaign finance law limiting corporate and union expenditures on advertising for or against political candidates was a violation of free speech rights. For the decision, the court invoked the doctrine of corporate personhood, a doctrine that since the 1800s has expanded corporate access to the rights of individuals as guaranteed by the U.S. Constitution. By further extending the right of free speech beyond individuals, the ruling lets corporate directors channel unlimited company funds toward promoting candidates favorable to their interests. Criminal law, meanwhile, has not been similarly extended to address corporate actions, which are instead primarily overseen via government regulations, despite the tremendous power corporate actors have to shape, weaken, and evade such regulations.

As the previous chapter laid out, the lack of effective measures for holding corporations accountable for their actions enabled the asbestos, lead, and tobacco industries to use the tactics of manufacturing doubt and uncertainty to keep their products on the market and avoid regulation, long after strong evidence of harm had been amassed. Indeed, corporate directors often enjoy political, economic, and cultural capital to minimize regulation: their positions of power and wealth afford them access far greater than that of the general public and small businesses to political representatives and decision-making processes, enabling them to wield influence through lobbyists, campaign contributions, and strategic appointments to governmental executive committees.[1] Corporate influence over regulations and law is evidenced by the fact that the deliberate manipulation of science has yet to be made illegal. It is difficult not only to institute effective regulation of corporations, but also to hold them accountable under criminal law. One cannot exactly throw a corporation into prison, regardless of its actions.

Given the disproportionate power of large businesses in determining regulation, and the difficulty of applying criminal law to a corporation, those hoping to hold the asbestos, lead, or tobacco industries accountable for their actions have filed lawsuits instead. Seeking both corporate accountability and compensation for harm, such lawsuits can be seen as a hybrid of criminal and common law, playing the dual role of controlling socially harmful behavior and compensating the injured.[2]

To stave off liability, defendant companies have fought against such lawsuits on a scale comparable to their battles against scientific research and regulation, again drawing upon the product defense industry (PDI) to discredit the suits by sowing doubt concerning the intentions of plaintiffs and their lawyers. As legal studies scholars have pointed out, law resides not just in the books but in the mind, manifesting as a set of attitudes, actions, and habits known as legal consciousness.[3] The asbestos, tobacco, and lead industries have used their influence to reshape our legal consciousness, reframing the lawsuits filed against them as a story of tort law gone mad, taken out of its historic bounds by greedy attorneys and activist judges, and requiring congressional, jury, and judicial limits on its scope. Questions regarding corporate impunity, meanwhile, become secondary or forgotten.[4] Further, radical departures from legal precedent to protect corporate interests are rarely portrayed as judicial activism.

Broadly speaking, tort law developed through common law judicial decisions, largely adopted in the United States from Britain, designed to compensate individuals for damages in order to restore social equilibrium.[5] Criminal law is made up of federal and state statutes enforced by the government, situating individual crimes as crimes against the entire community: "the people" versus the defendant. Criminal law is therefore seen as regulating acts offensive to the entire public body, as defined by the state. Although criminal law is often thought of as public and tort law as private, some have argued this binary is false, and that torts have always served as a type of privately enforced public law.[6] For example, American Tort Reform Association counsel Victor Schwartz argues that common law allows people "to use the tort system to stop quasi-criminal conduct that, while not illegal, is unreasonable given the circumstances and could cause injury to someone."[7]

Given the lack of regulations preceding the Industrial Revolution, people often protected themselves from industrial harms via common law. In particular, public and private nuisance laws, which prohibit acts that "unreasonably interfere" with the rights of others, were used in the early years of the Industrial Revolution as a form of zoning measure, to keep undesirable smells, sounds, and polluting emissions in more remote areas.[8] Such cases, however, involved situations in which the nuisance was demonstrable and concrete. When it came to industrial pollution cases that involved a more scientifically and thus legally ambiguous nuisance, judges were often reluctant to impede economic growth and industrial progress.[9] Many courts therefore prioritized industrial growth, much in line with the other two branches of government, downplaying industrial risks and harms in the name of progress.

The reluctance of some judges to regulate industries was aided by the nationwide proliferation of law firms. U.S. firms with four or more lawyers increased from 17 in 1872, to 87 in 1892, to 445 by 1913.[10] These firms provided a variety of services beyond litigation, helping stave off antitrust and other local regulations on corporate expansion and loosen restrictions on the issuance of stocks and bonds for investment. They also lobbied for state investment in a given company and against its taxation, and oversaw the expansion of growing industries like railroads and electricity into new economic areas, in the process often defeating or watering down local efforts at control.[11] Corporate lawyers also passed legislation limiting the scope of legal claims that could be filed by the public, seen as a precursor of "tort reform."[12] In short, these firms helped facilitate the growth of national corporations.

Further expanding corporate power was the legal recognition of corporations as artificial persons under the law. This was the result not of an actual court decision, but of headnotes written by legal clerk J. C. Bancroft Davis for the 1886 U.S. Supreme Court case *Santa Clara County v. Southern Pacific Railroad*. A former president of the Newburgh and New York Railroad, Davis wrote in his notes that the court was of the opinion that Fourteenth Amendment provisions—including conferred citizenship, due process, and equal protection rights—also applied to corporations. Such a statement cannot be found in the judge's actual decision. Regardless, *Santa Clara* was treated as legal precedent and helped extend individual rights to corporations, such as freedom of speech and due process.[13] By 1910, the Supreme Court had heard 288

Fourteenth Amendment cases addressing corporate rights, and only 19 addressing African American rights.[14]

Along with the weakening of state charters and the growth of corporate personhood came the legal concept of limited liability, which posited that business owners and shareholders should not be held legally accountable for corporate actions. Yet criminal law was shaped with the actions of individuals, not corporations, in mind and does not easily accommodate the way that more dispersed and indirect actions, such as neglect or deceit, can lead to harm or death. For example, deaths on a work site, regardless of cause, are often referred to as "accidents."[15]

This dynamic played out in the case of the asbestos industry. In the 1920s, workers exposed to asbestos began filing the first workers' compensation claims for lung diseases contracted on the job. Workers' compensation ensures a no-fault responsibility, allowing a worker to obtain compensation for medical costs while shielding corporations from liability. Unfortunately, compensation to asbestos victims was often inadequate, and some workers found themselves ineligible due to statutes of limitations, as the latency period for asbestos-related diseases is anywhere from ten to forty years.[16]

As evidence grew that asbestos was toxic and, worse, that asbestos manufacturers had known this, the industry tried to treat civil lawsuits much as they treated unfavorable science: with suppression. The companies moved to channel all legal claims into workers' compensation or out-of-court settlements, preventing publicly accessible trial records. As a condition of these out-of-court settlements, manufacturers demanded assurance from plaintiffs' lawyers that they would forgo all future asbestos suits and render confidential any evidence that had been obtained.[17] The early cases that reached trial were unsuccessful because plaintiffs could show no evidence proving that companies knew asbestos was harmful, prior to a widely publicized 1965 epidemiological study.[18]

The development of strict liability in 1965, which holds manufacturers responsible for "failure to warn" of an "unreasonably dangerous" product, allowed for suits against the sellers of asbestos products, not just the manufacturers, and the number of claims quickly grew.[19] By 1978, plaintiff lawyers came together to form the Asbestos Litigation Group, and through legal discovery—the fact-finding process prior to trial—they were able to succeed in releasing the "Sumner Simpson Papers." These internal industry documents showed asbestos manufacturers had funded research and found evidence of the link between asbestos and cancer, but had not disclosed the findings.[20] After the release of the papers, lawyers successfully argued that workers' compensation clauses should not shield asbestos manufacturers from fraud and conspiracy charges.[21]

Asbestos manufacturers then tried to settle most disputes out of court to avoid public exposure of large damages awards, which were occurring with greater frequency. In 1982, manufacturer Johns Manville filed for bankruptcy protection, resulting in the formation of a court-ordered trust to pay the company's claimants, still in operation today. Seventeen more companies filed for bankruptcy in the 1980s and another twenty-four in the 1990s, for a total of eighty by 2008.[22] After the declaration of bankruptcy, claims are stayed, leaving lawyers and administrators to negotiate the debts, usually involving formation of a trust to pay claimants through future profits and company insurers. Formation of a trust, however, can take years, and the trusts often go bankrupt. Meanwhile, companies can regroup and become profitable again, as was the case with Johns Manville. Bought by Warren Buffett's Berkshire Hathaway conglomerate in 2001, Johns Manville has once again become a lucrative business while its asbestos trust payments to claimants have dwindled to a few thousand dollars per person.[23] Asbestos-related claims are still piling up, and how all the medical costs will be paid remains a highly contentious issue.

During the asbestos trials, the tobacco industry was facing its own lawsuits but took a much more active stance in fighting them. Scholars have identified three waves of tobacco litigation.[24] In the first wave (1954–73) plaintiffs were hampered by a lack of medical studies establishing a clear link between smoking and disease, leading to difficulties in establishing causality, and allowing the industry to argue that smokers had freely chosen to smoke and thereby assumed the risk. The second wave (1983–92), seeking strict liability, was thwarted by the federal requirement for warning labels on cigarette packaging and advertising, which enabled defendant lawyers to argue that plaintiffs had chosen to smoke despite warnings. As in the case of asbestos, it was not until the public was made aware that the tobacco industry had known of the harms of smoking that a few suits proved successful. This marked the third wave of lawsuits, starting in the mid-'90s.

The first and second waves of tobacco lawsuits were also hampered by industry litigation overload: a well-financed, coordinated strategy to overwhelm plaintiff lawyers, sparing no cost to protect the multibillion-dollar industry.[25] As a 1988 memo from a lawyer for tobacco giant RJ Reynolds famously stated: "To quote General Patton, the way we won these cases was not by spending all of Reynolds' money, but by making that other son of a bitch spend all of his."[26] Of the more than seven hundred product liability lawsuits filed up to the mid-'90s, the sole case awarded compensation, *Cipollone v. Liggett Group* (1990), was later overturned on technical grounds; the plaintiff's firms declined to continue, as they had already spent a decade and millions of dollars on the case.[27] The case did result, however, in a 1992 Supreme Court decision that warning labels did not preempt liability—a common argument of tobacco lawyers.[28]

By the early 1990s, plaintiffs' lawyers had joined forces under the Tobacco Products Liability Program, aimed at transferring costs from injured parties to tobacco companies, raising public awareness, and gaining access to more industry documents through the discovery process.[29] These "cause lawyers" linked up with product liability lawyers who had knowledge and resources from fighting asbestos cases, in a conscious strategic effort to overcome the structural advantages of defendant law firms as already established legal players.[30]

In 1994, the class action suit *Castano v. American Tobacco Co. et al.* was filed, as was the first state Medicaid suit for reimbursement of the public costs of smoking-related illness. Within three years, attorneys general from forty other states had filed lawsuits. In 1996, Liggett Group, facing financial difficulty and fearing a guilty verdict in *Castano*, broke ranks and agreed to settle.[31] That same year a jury also awarded $750,000 to lung cancer patient Grady Carter, the first jury to rule against tobacco after *Cipollone*. In 1997 other tobacco companies settled the state medical cost reimbursement suits of Mississippi, Florida, and Texas, leading to the 1998 national settlement of $246 billion.

The development of tobacco and other toxic tort suits, as well as medical malpractice suits, generated renewed calls for "tort reform," an effort tobacco companies began heavily supporting and funding. Among the groups the tobacco industry funded in its efforts to narrow public legal rights was the Washington Legal Foundation, established in 1977, which produces studies and media reports in support of liability limits. Internal tobacco documents at the Legacy Tobacco Documents Library show that, between 1995 and 1999, Philip Morris gave the Washington Legal Foundation more than one million dollars. To-bacco companies also funded a group calling itself Citizens for a Sound Economy, which in 1995 spent millions of dollars on an ad campaign to portray torts as a burden to consumers.[32]

In addition, internal tobacco documents detail how the industry launched its own tort-narrowing efforts, at a budget of more than $17 million in 1995 alone, and enlisted the participation of other indus-tries to limit public access to the court system and compensation.[33] As part of the project, the public relations firm APCO helped fund and in some cases even start up "grassroots" citizens groups across the coun-try called Citizens Against Lawsuit Abuse.[34] Creating a model that was then replicated nationwide, the Texas Citizens Against Lawsuit Abuse groups developed a statewide support network that included the Texas Chamber of Commerce, the Texas Public Policy Founda-tion, and numerous corporations wanting to shield themselves from consumer lawsuits. Other Citizens Against Lawsuit Abuse groups pushed for state limits on liability, such as abolishing punitive dam-ages, capping compensatory damages, reducing lawyers' contingency fees, and limiting class action suits and the applicability of certain legal rules.

Tobacco companies also moved to influence judges directly by funding organizations that sponsor judicial seminars, such as Libertad Inc., solely funded by Philip Morris, which has recruited lawyers, busi-ness executives, and politicians to speak about the tobacco industry at paid seminars.[35] Although many have argued such industry-funded "ju-dicial education" events should not be allowed, they are still legal, raising questions about possible undue influence over judicial opinions. Chief Justice John Roberts, who in 2008 reduced the punitive damages for Exxon over the *Valdez* oil spill, in 2006 served on the advisory council of

the Law and Economic Center at George Mason and attended its judicial seminars, despite the center's heavy funding by oil and tobacco corporations, including Exxon.[36] *Daubert v.
Merrell Dow Pharmaceuticals*, the 1993 Supreme Court case that changed the standard of legally permissible scientific testimony from "general acceptance in the relevant field" to the judge's discretion,[37] was first drawn upon by Ninth Circuit judge Alex Kozinski, who had attended a Libertad Inc. seminar.[38] *Daubert* enables defendants' lawyers to question the legitimacy of even established scientists as expert witnesses,[39] and allows judges to determine admissible expertise regardless of their own qualifications for making such determinations.

Recently, it was discovered that corporate rights meetings organized by Koch Industries, the second-largest private company in the United States, were attended by Supreme Court Justices Scalia and Thomas before they helped undo limits on corporate election spending in the 2010 *Citizens United* decision.[40] Koch Industries went on to pump millions into the 2010 midterm elections, partly through an organization called Americans for Prosperity, a large funder of Tea Party movements, many of whose members advocate further limiting government oversight over corporate affairs.[41]

While tobacco focused on limiting liability and fighting scientific testimony, former lead paint manufacturers have helped alter the body of law itself. Through consultant services, the lead industry recruited conservative lawyers to write very narrow interpretations of tort law that framed limited corporate liability as "traditional" common law. These interpretations were then published as op-eds, newspaper articles, and papers in legal journals. In trials involving lead paint, these same narrow legal interpretations were adopted and even cited by state Supreme Courts to shield former manufacturers from liability.

As discussed, the lead industry responded to the research indicating that lead paint posed a hazard to human health by questioning the findings, blaming the children affected, and encouraging the use of lead paint in public buildings and housing. In 1970, federal legislation called for abating existing lead paint hazards, but little funding was appropriated for this purpose.[42] The federal government offered grants to cities and states to help property owners pay for removing lead paint, and some states passed laws making removal a requirement. Such laws, however, have been unevenly enforced and implemented, resulting in poor urban areas being more likely to contain properties with lead hazards.[43]

To deal with inadequate removal, lawsuits were generally targeted at landlords and property owners, who were portrayed in regulation as legally responsible for abating the hazard. Growing awareness of the lead industry's misinformation campaign, however, led in 1987 to the first lawsuit against several former lead paint manufacturers, with other suits soon following. Many early claims were dismissed because of the difficulty of identifying specific manufacturers with lead hazards, but community organizations continued to push for accountability, emboldened in part by the waves of asbestos and tobacco litigation.

In 1999, the State of Rhode Island brought a suit against several former lead pigment producers, arguing the collective presence of lead paint in the state constituted a public nuisance that interfered with the general public's health and safety, and that defendant companies had knowingly and substantially contributed to the nuisance and were liable for abatement. Several states and cities soon followed with similar suits claiming public nuisance and fraud, civil conspiracy, and unjust enrichment. In the lead paint trials, plaintiff lawyers argued the companies or their predecessors had continued to manufacture lead pigment long after they had realized the danger, submitting internal documents from DuPont, the Lead Industries Association, Sherwin-Williams, and others unearthed in earlier lawsuits as evidence.[44] They also submitted records on the number of children harmed and poisoned due to the contamination. Defendant companies were shocked when juries in New Jersey and Rhode Island found them liable.

The success of these suits alarmed other companies concerned about the increasing use and effectiveness of public nuisance claims. As stated in the 1979 *Restatement (Second) of Torts*, public nuisance is defined as "an unreasonable interference with a right common to the general public." To have legal standing to bring a public nuisance claim within federal court, plaintiffs must show that they have an "injury in fact" that is actual or imminent and not merely hypothetical, is fairly traceable to the challenged action of the defendant, and is likely to be redressed by a favorable decision.[45] The broad applicability of the doctrine made it a source of alarm for defendant companies, in particular given the growing technological advances in scientific research and its increasing practice beyond corporate control.

In 1989, a chemical manufacturing company was found liable under the public nuisance doctrine for the contamination of the Love Canal landfill site forty years earlier. In the 1990s, forty states also alleged public nuisance in their suits against tobacco. While such claims arguably remained within the public nuisance principle as articulated in the *Restatement of Torts*, namely that those who substantially contribute to the creation or maintenance of a nuisance are liable,[46] pro-business groups decried the claims as distortions of traditional common law, arguing public nuisance was moving far beyond its intended legal application.

Critics included lawyers Donald Gifford and Victor Schwartz. Gifford argued that public nuisance had inappropriately become akin to a mass products liability tort,[47] Schwartz that it had lost the required element of control: that only those presently able to abate a nuisance, such as property owners, are liable.[48] Both Gifford and Schwartz criticized the Rhode Island jury decision in journal articles, which is not surprising given that both are tied to the industry. Schwartz is general counsel to the American Tort Reform Association and works for the firm Shook, Hardy, Bacon, which has represented lead companies in litigation. Gifford has been a consultant for former lead paint manufacturers including DuPont, a defendant in the Rhode Island cases. He also served as chair of the Maryland Lead Paint Poisoning Commission from 1992 until 1995 and helped shape the state's lead prevention laws holding property owners, rather than former lead paint manufacturers, legally accountable for lead abatement. Therefore, while their critique of the Rhode Island jury's decision was to be expected, what was surprising was that the Supreme Courts of New Jersey and particularly Rhode Island heavily relied upon and cited their articles in overturning the juries' decisions, helping transform state law in the process.

In 2007, the Supreme Court of New Jersey found that public nuisance claims could not be used in a lead paint case brought by more than twenty counties and cities (re Lead Paint Litigation), followed by the Supreme Court of Rhode Island in 2008 (State of R.I. v. Lead Industries Association). Drawing upon Gifford and Schwartz in its opinion, the Supreme Court of New Jersey argued that "were we to find a cause of action here, 'nuisance law' would become a monster that would devour in one gulp the entire law of tort."[49] The court drew upon the Restatement (Second) of Torts for the definition of public nuisance as "unreasonable interference with a right common to the general public," but a few pages later stated that "a public nuisance, by definition, is related to conduct, performed in a location within the actor's control, which has an adverse effect on a common right," echoing the Schwartz paper (coauthored by P. Goldberg) without citing where this definition or element of control had come from, which the court nevertheless went on to label "time-honored."[50] The Rhode Island court, in contrast, directly cited Gifford for this requirement: "Liability for nuisance—both public and private—is premised not on the creation of a nuisance but rather on the defendant's current control of the instrumentality causing the nuisance"[51] and Schwartz and Goldberg: "[F]urnishing a product or instrumentality—whether it be chemicals, asbestos, guns, lead paint, or other products is not the same as having control over that instrumentality,"[52] as well as an obscure article by Mark P. Gagliardi: "There must be some control over the instrumentality alleged to have created the nuisance."[53] To be sure, the Rhode Island court cited three state district cases that mention control, but did not discuss the multiple public nuisance cases that do not, instead relying heavily upon these few articles to frame control as a legal requirement. Under the New Jersey and Rhode Island courts' reading, since former lead paint manufacturers do not presently "control" the premises containing lead hazards, meaning they do not own the buildings, they are not liable—a decision deliberately ignoring the evidence suggesting that the companies knowingly created the nuisance in the first place.

When asked whether citing industry representatives was unusual, a lawyer for the plaintiffs in the Rhode Island case, Bob McConnell, said, "I don't recall ever seeing an appellate court rely on law review articles by paid industry experts. That was a new one for me." He was dismayed that now, by the court's logic, "once you give up control of the premises you pollute and the polluting product, you escape all liability for the public nuisance."[54]

Having worked on asbestos and tobacco cases, another plaintiff lawyer on the case, McConnell's brother Jack, observed, "Tobacco companies never really had a good political spin for all the things they did, neither did asbestos companies. Whereas lead hired PR firms to try and spin it a certain way, and what they spun was a feeling that it was 'unfair' to hold the manufacturers of a legal product so long ago responsible for these injuries."[55] Indeed, a LexisNexis special report on the Rhode Island case is advertised as chronicling "the history of a landmark lawsuit against an industry that made a legal product and then discontinued it according to federal regulations, only to be sued after the fact."[56] The legal dismissal of these cases has allowed the aggressive marketing and misinformation campaigns of certain lead paint companies to be framed as another example of "tort abuse," appropriately beaten back. The harms, in turn, are suffered and paid for by the public.

The next section focuses specifically on global warming, looking first at the dynamics of the fossil fuel industry and tracing how it has drawn upon many of the tactics discussed: creating scientific doubt, delaying government regulation, and affecting legal and judicial consciousness, exposing growing numbers of people to potential harm. How will regulation and liability play out when an industry as powerful as fossil fuels takes advantage of persuasive PDI tactics, particularly for a threat as severe as global climate change?

KIVALINA, BY NATURAL EROSION at first, began shrinking. A fifty-year study by the National Oceanic and Atmospheric Administration (NOAA) showed that what had started out as an island of fifty-five acres in 1953 had become only twenty-seven acres of livable space by 2003, all for a growing population. In 1990, Cecil Hawley, then tribal administrator, wrote a letter to the City of Kivalina that was received by me as city administrator, raising the issue of relocating the people of the village. Hawley's letter addressed the issue because the people of Kivalina had been discussing the lack of water and sewage services, the minimal residential space, and the lack of jobs, as well as the land erosion. Thus began the discussion of relocating the entire community.

— KIVALINA TRIBAL ADMINISTRATOR COLLEEN SWAN

THREE

FOSSIL FUELS AND U.S. POWER

Coal, oil, and natural gas are called fossil fuels because they are formed from layers of carbon-based organic matter that had been plants and simple marine creatures millions of years ago. Through chemical processes, the energy these life forms absorbed from the sun becomes transformed, allowing us to dig them up and use them as a form of concentrated, fossilized fuel. The United States was built upon and centers on their use: according to the U.S. Department of Energy, fossil fuels provide 85 percent of U.S. energy.[1]

Fossil fuel industries grew up alongside and literally fueled U.S. development, and established themselves as "natural" monopolies. In doing so, they created powerful, overlapping ties with large manufacturers, financial institutions, and the military-industrial complex. They also have strong ties to the U.S. government: while fossil fuel companies often claim to want limited governmental regulation of their industries based on free-market principles, such arguments ignore how many government representatives serve, overlap with, or come directly from the fossil fuel industry, and have helped anchor fossil fuel use for over a century, both domestically and globally.[2]

Fossil fuels currently serve as the basis for the creation of most industrial products and the financial instruments derived from them, as well as the mass production of weapons, making fossil fuels central to the current world order and any transition away from them a huge threat to many powerful interests. Yet while fossil fuel companies assert the use of fossil fuels benefits the United States as a whole, most of the benefits accrue to a small group of transnational actors across various energy, industrial, military, and financial sectors, whose power and influence over the U.S. government were further cemented during the George W. Bush administration.

COAL

Coal begins as decaying plant matter, called peat. Peat bogs form from layers of trees and plants that decay and sink, primarily along wetlands and river valleys. If peat is rapidly buried under layers of mud and sand before fully decaying, it retains the carbon the plants captured from the sun. The matter is then broken down by anaerobic material that thrives without oxygen. Over time, heat and pressure compress the organic matter and squeeze out the moisture, concentrating the carbon, a process that takes millions of years. A chunk of coal contains virtually every element in the periodic table, but primarily carbon, and the ratio of the elements to carbon determines both its energy and its pollution output. While coal may hark back to the early days of the Industrial Revolution, it continues to play a central role in daily U.S. life, primarily in the production of electricity. In the United States, more than a billion tons of coal are burned per year, accounting for about 40 percent of U.S. carbon dioxide emissions.[3] The United States has by far more estimated recoverable coal reserves than any other country, and the use of coal is accelerating globally.

The ten largest coal companies extract about 60 percent of U.S. coal, with the next ten extracting an additional 30 percent,[4] creating a consortium of controlling companies sometimes referred to as Big Coal.[5] The largest coal producer is Peabody Energy Corporation, comprising nearly 17 percent of U.S. coal extraction.[6] It is interesting to note that the companies refer to their business as coal "production" since they do not so much produce coal as hire people to dig it up and burn it, while fighting against ownership of its polluting emissions.[7] Although we might think of coal companies as individual corporations, ownership often overlaps with large financial institutions: Peabody, for example, was bought by Lehman Merchant Banking Partners in 1998,[8] which retained 59 percent interest in the company after it went public in 2001. Although Lehman filed for bankruptcy in 2008, Peabody is still enjoying large profits, and over its history has evolved from a coal company to an energy company, investing in coal-powered plants and buying other power companies and mines, domestically and overseas.

Coal mining began in the United States in the early 1700s, and had become a commercial venture by the 1730s. Many areas where coal was surveyed were quickly claimed by mining companies and railroads, which together monopolized the resource.[9] Throughout mining history, various methods of surface or underground mining have been used, depending upon the depth of the coal's location. Early miners worked in dangerous conditions, subjected to various hazards from explosions, falling debris, and lung disease due to coal dust inhalation, which led to movements for unionization and increased worker protections.[10] Although the movements were fairly successful, lax regulation and long-term exposure leaves the coal miners of today still subject to many hazards, particularly pneumoconiosis, an irreversible, debilitating respiratory disease from regularly inhaling coal dust, also known as black lung.[11] Miners are also still subject to disasters: in April 2010, twenty-nine workers were killed in an explosion in a West Virginia coal mine owned by Massey Energy, which had a long history of safety violations. Federal mine safety officials later faulted Massey for insufficient oversight, which the officials believe led to a buildup of coal dust in the mine that set the stage for the explosion.

Many areas of the United States rich in coal have low economic growth, in line with the "resource curse."[12] Control over natural resources can become centralized, leaving these areas dependent upon the revenues and highly susceptible to price fluctuations, simultaneously crowding out other sources of development.[13] Mining companies continue to argue that the industry brings jobs and economic growth to an area, but research points in the opposite direction. Comprehensive analysis of published, nonmetropolitan mining data show a statistically significant correlation between mining and unemployment and poverty.[14] The correlation is particularly strong for the U.S. East, which was established as a coal mining area earlier than the West, and was unable to institute more economic concessions for local residents, such as Wyoming's Permanent Mineral Trust Fund. In coal-rich areas of the East, pockets of great coal wealth exist alongside some of the highest levels of poverty, unemployment, and health problems in the nation.[15] The social costs include the power and influence of coal over local, state, and federal development decisions: coal companies can lobby for and help tip the balance in favor of coal-friendly representatives, legislation, and even judges, influence that can now expand after the 2010 *Citizens United* decision.

Residents of coal mining areas must also deal with the environmental and health consequences, the costs of which are often externalized, or paid for by the public, in terms of both medical costs and lower quality of life and mental well-being.[16] The effects of coal mining include deforestation, flooding, mudslides, and the fouling of headwater streams. Once mined, the coal and rock removed (ore) is mixed with water and transported in pipelines for processing, with the leftover waste, or coal sludge, stored indefinitely in impoundments, such as large dams up to hundreds of feet high. In 1972, a coal sludge impoundment failed in Buffalo Creek, West Virginia, flooding out and killing 125 people and leaving 4,000 homeless, while a 2008 "spill" near Kingston, Tennessee, released an estimated one billion gallons of sludge, flooding homes and polluting rivers.[17] Coal waste has also been found to leach into drinking water, contaminating it with carcinogenic chemicals used in processing and toxic heavy metals. Those metals include mercury, with coal-fired power plants the largest source of mercury releases in the United States.[18] According to a 2009 *New York Times* analysis of EPA data, power plants are the nation's biggest producer of toxic waste, surpassing industries such as plastic or paint manufacturing and chemical plants.[19] Old mines can catch fire and burn for decades, or flood and disgorge acid mine water.[20] Coal mining also accounts for approximately 10 percent of current U.S. releases of methane.[21]

To expedite coal extraction, some coal companies in the 1990s began blasting away the tops of mountains. This practice, called mountaintop removal, uses the same mixture of ammonium nitrate and fuel oil that, as author Jeff Goodell notes, Timothy McVeigh used for the Oklahoma City bombing.[22] Mountaintop removal unearths hundreds of feet of forest, topsoil, and sandstone, with the unused debris—categorized as "fill" to make the practice legal—pushed down into valleys and streams.[23] According to a 2005 EPA Environmental Impact Statement, over seven hundred miles of Appalachian streams were buried from 1985 to 2001.[24]

Although the EPA tightened regulations on such dumping in April 2010, one month later the agency green-lighted the filling of three valleys; then, in January 2011, the agency vetoed a water permit for what would have been the largest mountaintop removal operation in the United States (Spruce 1 mine), showing the issue is far from settled. The groups Climate Ground Zero and Coal River Mountain Watch have done studies suggesting many areas currently subjected to mountaintop removal would gain more revenues and jobs with wind farms, particularly once the environmental and health costs of the coal production process are factored in.[25] Pro-coal politicians, meanwhile, have repeatedly filed legal challenges against the EPA regarding any regulatory measures directed at coal and mountaintop removal, suits that are apparently exempt from conservative opposition to "lawsuit abuse."

Native Americans also have a long history of dealing with the health and environmental consequences of coal mining. Early acts and treaties between the federal government and Native Americans allowed for the U.S. extraction of minerals, oil, and coal on reservations, although many tribes have successfully fought and renegotiated treaty terms.[26] Royalties often fail to reach tribal members, however, due to government and corporate corruption as well as state and tribal mismanagement.[27] Thus despite living in areas rich with natural resources, Native Americans are among the poorest people in the United States,[28] a trend seen globally among indigenous populations and leading to transnational movements for access to natural resources, autonomy, and a healthy environment.[29]

Coal was and continues to be—next to oil—central to literally powering modern development. Coal was heavily used by the British to ramp up their industrial revolution. Coal helped mass-produce steel, setting off a new wave of industrial activities. Coal-powered steam engines motored ships and railroads, further integrating markets across vast geographic areas and spurring the growth of large consumer goods industries.[30] And today, most coal is used to generate electricity.[31]

While Thomas Edison is often credited with having built the first electric grid in 1882, there were already small-scale generators of electricity in pockets of Britain and the United States.[32] Edison did not want to sell generators, however; he wanted to sell electricity, and set up centralized plants and power lines to service a large area while controlling generation, transmission, and distribution.[33] Investor J. P. Morgan was interested in Edison's technology, as was railroad tycoon Henry Villard, and together they created Edison General Electric, which over time became General Electric (GE).[34]

Making electricity a centralized, privatized commodity was not a natural or inevitable occurrence. There was a question as to whether it would be a public service, like water.[35] By the late 1800s, hundreds of municipalities had voted on bonds to build power generators and grids at per-cost rates.[36] Private utilities saw this as a threat to potential profits, and in 1905 several representatives of the power sector came together for a commission to discuss public power. After two years, the commission recommended that private power companies push for state regulation of their industry, to install themselves as a monopoly and make regulators natural allies, while staving off the momentum for local control.[37]

The U.S. government had a national interest in establishing a stable supply of electricity for the country's military and industrial sectors, in particular for World War I manufacturing needs.[38] By 1910, power companies had been placed under the supervision of state commissions. Notoriously understaffed and underfunded, regulatory agencies were faced with the difficult and arguably contradictory task of servicing both the needs of consumers and the power industry, all within a political atmosphere tipped toward the latter.[39] Although President

Roosevelt's New Deal offered some funding for bringing electricity to more remote areas and helped build up rural electric cooperatives,[40] many other public electric utilities struggled after the Great Depression and were subsequently bought up by larger power companies.[41]

With growing profits and lax regulation, the ownership of private utilities became concentrated in fewer and fewer hands. By the 1920s, sixteen interrelated holding companies provided 85 percent of the electricity in the United States.[42] Energy investors often had overlapping interests in oil, finance, and manufacturing, and would consolidate their divergent interests into holding companies, drawing upon the advice of economic and legal experts to expand their shares in other companies.[43] Edison's protégé Samuel Insull built up an empire of 248 companies, including coal, railroads, and construction.[44] Other holding companies were owned by financiers, with the power industry providing one-third of all corporate financing in the 1920s.[45] The complexity and opaqueness of the industry's reach made it ideal for attracting investors, through both stocks sold by brokers and stock sold directly to the public via mail campaigns for individual "customer ownership."[46] These small-scale investors were left with worthless stocks and bonds when Wall Street crashed in 1929.

After the crash, public pressure led to the 1935 Public Utility Holding Company Act to break up the holding companies. The act prevented the parent or holding company from speculating in other industries with ratepayers' money. In addition, the act scaled down the geographic scope of the service areas, giving utilities monopoly in a region in exchange for regulated rates, instituted at the local level and overseen by the Federal Energy Regulatory Commission (FERC). The act was amended ten times between 1936 and 1966, often in ways that created loopholes in the antitrust regulation.[47]

During the oil crises of the 1970s, prices for electricity shot up, and public pressure led to a government investigation into the power industry, which found interlocking directorates and stock concentrations reminiscent of the 1920s holding companies. The investigation, however, was undercut by President Reagan, who installed FERC administrators that openly disdained regulation, with some arguing that the Public Utility Holding Company Act should be repealed altogether.[48]

In the 1990s, power companies such as Enron pushed for electricity deregulation so they could enter the market. This eventually led to the breakup of vertically integrated electric industries that had dealt with energy from its generation to its transmission and distribution, opening up the market for energy producers and traders. Enron, in particular, was able to push for such deregulation in both energy trading and derivatives by drawing upon CEO Ken Lay's connections to Senator Phil Gramm and then Texas governor, later U.S. president, George W. Bush.[49] FERC caps on generation prices were removed, and energy generation was sold as a tradable commodity on a national scale, open to any states that deregulated.[50]

A secondary, derivatives market also developed to reduce, or hedge against, the risks in energy trading.[51] Derivatives are financial products whose value derives from an underlying asset, and can be used conservatively as a form of risk management or more liberally as a means of market speculation—trading with the objective of achieving profits through the successful anticipation of price movements. Various forms of financial derivatives had proliferated by the 1990s, and were largely shielded from government regulation.[52] The Commodities Future Modernization Act (CFMA) of 2000, heavily lobbied for by Enron personnel, codified the exemption of derivative products such as credit default swaps and collateralized debt obligations that created the financial bubble leading up to the 2008 financial collapse. CFMA also included what became known as the "Enron loophole," exempting most energy trades between two parties ("over-the-counter"), as well as trades on electronic energy markets.[53]

By 2000, energy brokers and electronic energy trading had prolifer-ated, as companies could speculate on this market without even owning a power station.[54] The growth in speculation and lack of regulation helped provide the opaqueness for Enron to inflate its value through en-ergy and credit derivatives and place seventh on *Fortune*'s 2000 list of the largest companies in the world, despite producing so little of any con-crete value.[55] Although it certainly tried, Enron eventually could not beat back the increasing questions regarding its rapid and seemingly in-explicable growth, and the company declared bankruptcy in 2001.

Nevertheless, the company's efforts laid the groundwork for the further centralization of control over energy, and the increased fusion of the energy industry with the financial sector. Control over energy generation became concentrated in fewer hands, as public utilities were encouraged to sell their generating facilities and focus instead on transmission and distribution. By 2000, private utilities owned over 80 percent of U.S. generation capacity,[56] and the top twenty U.S. power companies supplied over half the nation's electricity market.[57]

By the early 2000s, large financial institutions, pension funds, hedge funds—investment funds with diverse portfolios spanning stocks, bonds, and commodities—and other investment funds were pouring billions into energy commodities (natural gas, crude oil, and electricity) and energy futures markets to try to capitalize on price changes or hedge against them.[58] A 2006 Senate report on rising oil and gas prices noted that financial speculators had made perhaps hun-dreds of millions of dollars in profits through trading in energy commodities. The exact value was not known, however, since much of the market was outside government oversight.[59] These trades can artificially inflate demand and thus price,[60] such as for oil through large purchases of oil futures contracts.[61]

Those who pushed for energy deregulation argued that regulation stunts development, creating little incentive to innovate. The innovation, however, appears to have mainly taken place in finance and trading, not actual energy production. Through deregulation and growing profits, coal still accounts for about half of U.S. electricity needs, just as it did in the 1970s.[62] Using existing coal-fired plants makes economic sense for the industry, as the cost of using them is cheaper for power companies than drawing upon newer, cleaner technologies, since so many of the environmental and health costs are passed on to the public.[63] A 2011 Harvard study led by Dr. Paul Epstein found that accounting for the full costs of coal, such as health expenses and environmental damages, would double to triple its price.[64] The use of old coal plants is a particularly strong contributor to air pollution, as many plants built before the Clean Air Act amendments of 1977 are not subject to the controls of the act unless undergoing "major modifications," creating a perverse incentive to maintain rather than upgrade or replace them.[65] As of early 2011, the EPA is considering new and tighter regulations on such pollutants as coal waste, mercury, and particulate matter, which is driving some coal plant owners to consider retiring rather than upgrading their existing power stations.

While most natural gas plants emit fewer pollutants and about half as much carbon dioxide as coal plants, the gas is primarily composed of methane, which has been found to leak out during gas production and distribution.[66] In early 2011, the EPA drew upon the most recent data for the natural gas industry and doubled the estimate of the methane release from the life cycle of natural gas production. Depleted gas reserves are leading companies to turn to unconventional sources requiring increased energy to reach, such as deeply buried sedimentary rock, or shale. Shale is fractured to release the gas in its pores, a chemical- and water-intensive process, called "fracking," that has been reported to pollute local drinking water supplies and has led to public calls for tighter regulations.[67] Building up an infrastructure for imported liquefied natural gas, meanwhile, would be very costly due to the difficulty involved in its chemical transformation and safe transport.[68]

Many power companies have been looking to expand the use of coal plants, both internationally and domestically. The amount of coal exported by the United States is going up, rising from 59 million tons in 2007 to 81 million in 2008, primarily to Asia.[69] Although the 2008 economic crash caused a decline in 2009 exports, the amount of exports rebounded to 81.5 million tons in 2010, and is expected to jump in 2011. Power companies such as AES, the Southern Company, and Peabody are acquiring and building up coal plants and mines overseas, sometimes amid widespread opposition from local populations facing displacement.[70] The power industry is also looking to maintain its U.S. market share through "clean coal" technology to sequester and store carbon dioxide, a process that, as a 2010 U.S. Government Accountability Office report noted, is technologically unproven on a long-term scale, expensive, and risky.[71] Nevertheless, it is financially supported by the U.S. Department of Energy, which is also funding the conversion of coal into synthetic gas, again in the name of "clean coal."

This ossification of the social use of coal has implications for U.S. national policy on climate change: congressional representatives from states dependent upon coal are far more likely to vote against federal and state-level proposals to reduce greenhouse gas emissions than those who are not.[72] Increasing grassroots opposition to coal has made coal plants a riskier investment, prompting many financial institutions to adopt a set of "carbon principles" to guide new investments, for instance, prioritizing projects in energy efficiency, renewable power, and carbon capture and storage. Such principles, however, represent more ideals than actions, and address neither the use of existing coal plants nor the growing profits from energy and energy derivatives trading. In response, activist organizations are pressuring financial institutions to stop funding new coal plants and mines, and there are growing calls for cities and states to phase out existing plants and move toward new energy sources under local control.[73] Although local-owned electricity sources could be a big step toward instituting alternatives to coal and natural gas, the United States is still heavily dependent on oil.

OIL

Petroleum (Latin for "rock oil") provides nearly half of U.S. energy needs, with transportation fuels responsible for about one-third of U.S. carbon dioxide emissions.[74] While most oil is used for gasoline, the by-products are broken down to provide the raw materials for many synthetic products, including plastics. Petroleum and its by-products are found in roads, medicine, cosmetics, food packaging, appliances, clothes, detergents, and pesticides, among other things. Indeed, it is hard to think of a market good that does not involve oil in some aspect of its production. The U.S. military is the single largest consumer of oil, with weapons like the F-15 fighter jet burning more oil in one hour than the average U.S. household consumes in a year.[75]

Oil forms much like coal, but the organic matter it comes from was primarily water life—zooplankton, algae, and bacteria that were buried very quickly under sand and silt and deprived of oxygen. Increasing temperature, pressure, and anaerobic material act upon the organic matter and, over millions of years, transform it into hydrocarbons. Since animal life (even simple creatures such as plankton) contains fat, oil is fluid, in contrast to coal, and is often found in layers of water, oil, and natural gas. The resulting liquid pools into porous rock or collects under layers of hard rock or dried sea salt, and gravitates upward, causing it to sometimes seep out naturally or gush out when drilled.

According to Ida Tarbell's *History of the Standard Oil Company*, published in 1904, oil was periodically found on the surfaces of springs and used as kerosene in lamps until the beginning of the nineteenth century.[76] Then in Kentucky, West Virginia, Ohio, and Pennsylvania, people drilling for salt hit instead upon a dark green substance, recognized as "rock oil." As the many uses of oil were being realized, Colonel Edwin Drake was sent by the Pennsylvania Rock Oil Company in 1859 to Titusville, Pennsylvania, the site of several crude oil seeps. After many fruitless attempts to increase the oil flow from the seeps, Drake decided to drill using techniques similar to salt wells, and struck oil.[77] Shortly thereafter, Tarbell's father moved the family to Titusville, hoping to profit from the new discovery. Soon the race was on to buy up land, find oil, and refine it for market use.[78]

Drawing upon the money he had made selling supplies to the U.S. government during the Civil War, John D. Rockefeller started buying up refineries, purposely undercutting competitors' prices to drive them out of business. He also negotiated exclusive shipping deals with railroads, and by 1879 controlled 90 percent of U.S. oil refining.[79] Rockefeller's Standard Oil was consolidated as a trust in 1882, to put its different branches under a single leadership, and its large reach and influence helped the company control oil supply and thus price.[80] Standard Oil eventually became a holding company, moving into iron, coal, shipping, and banking by 1899 (as Chase Manhattan Bank), with Rockefeller sitting on the board of nearly forty corporations.[81]

The growing and monopolizing power of Standard Oil was made public through Tarbell's investigative writings on the company, eventually leading to public demand for the Sherman Anti-Trust Act of 1890. The act did not define monopoly or what constituted illegal actions, however, leaving that to the courts to decide.[82] Seeing few changes enacted, states challenged Rockefeller's power in court, and in 1911 the Supreme Court ruled that Standard Oil was an unlawful trust and had six months to dissolve.[83]

As the company was put in charge of its own dissolution, however, it formed thirty-four separate companies, but with the same executives and owners.[84] Its growth expanded as ships and railroads increasingly turned toward oil. The power of the industry grew even more quickly with the invention of the Ford Model T, originally designed to run on ethanol but gradually switched to gasoline as the harsh impacts on crop yields during the Dust Bowl of the 1930s helped oil companies undercut ethanol prices and establish a market for themselves.[85] Automotive industries also invested in public electric railways, such as streetcar systems, only to dismantle them, moving to replace rail with buses, roads, and gas stations.[86] Today in the United States transportation accounts for two out of every three barrels of oil consumed, and the auto industry was until quite recently considered the backbone of the nation, having created the government-industry-worker model of mass production known as Fordism, and enabling the rise of suburbia. By midcentury, thirteen of the sixteen largest U.S. corporations were in oil or automobiles.[87]

War was also a big boost to the oil industry, as using oil offered a competitive edge in combat by making transportation faster and weapons more efficient. During World War I, the Oil Division of the U.S. Fuel Administration encouraged increases in oil production for military use, helping recentralize Standard Oil operations and push antitrust considerations to the side.[88] After the war, European nations divided the Middle East into spheres of influence, and the U.S. government pressured Britain to open up Iraq to U.S.-owned Standard of New Jersey and Socony.[89] Over time, the United States, Britain, and the Netherlands created an international oil cartel known as the Seven Sisters: Esso (later Exxon); Socal (later Chevron); Royal Dutch Shell; Anglo-Persian Oil Company (later BP); Socony (later Mobil); Gulf Oil (later BP and Chevron); and Texaco (also later Chevron), with all but the British/Dutch-owned Shell containing or later absorbing companies formed from the breakup of Standard Oil.[90] Together, the Seven Sisters were able to control the production and price of oil on the world market, leaving refining and less prosperous pockets of oil production to smaller domestic companies.[91] In the United States, officials in the oil industry had such a tight network overseas and wielded so much power and influence they publicly considered themselves instruments of national security and foreign policy.[92]

Largely left out of the oil arrangement were Germany and Japan, and their plans to secure their own reserves are seen as large factors in the invasion of Russia and bombing of Pearl Harbor, respectively—Germany to get at the oil-rich fields in the Caucasus Mountains, and Japan to try to immobilize the U.S. fleet as the country moved toward the East Indies.[93] The attack on Pearl Harbor, however, served to launch the U.S. entrance into World War II. The Allied powers went on to use an estimated seven billion barrels of oil, increasing the ties of the

U.S. government to the oil industry, as well as to sectors of manufacturing and finance, which helped provide the money and resources for military operations.[94] This relationship continued and strengthened after the war, developing into what President Eisenhower later termed a military-industrial complex, a merger of government and business interests around weapons and conflict.[95] By the end of the war, the United States had emerged as the world's undisputed superpower, cemented by the Allied nations' 1944 Bretton Woods agreement, which established the U.S. dollar as the world's reserve currency.[96] President Roosevelt also met with the king of Saudi Arabia in 1945 and made an agreement that exists to this day: Saudi Arabia would provide the United States with oil, and the United States would use its military to counter any threats to Saudi Arabia.[97] To further maintain global influence, the United States set up a network of overseas military bases,[98] many overlapping with those of the former British Empire.[99] Domestically, the government funded emerging industries such as electronics, aerospace, and information technology, fueling a period of rapid post-WWII industrial growth.[100] This model of industrialization, consumerism, and modern development was exported throughout the world.

All this activity depended on the heavy use of oil. By 1950, the United States produced half the world's oil,[101] and the U.S. military had become the world's single-largest oil purchaser, a distinction that continues to this day.[102] However, although the Seven Sisters dominated market share, and the United States had secured itself a large overseas supply, the companies did not necessarily have full control over the resource, as soon became apparent with two major events: peak oil, and the increasing nationalization of oil industries.

In 1956, geologist M. King Hubbert predicted U.S. oil production would soon peak. "Peak oil" refers to the point at which oil extraction reaches its maximum output and then declines, as it requires more energy and resources to reach the remaining oil than would be gained from extracting it.[103] Hubbert, an employee of Shell, noted that continental U.S. discovery had peaked in the 1930s, and figured production would have to do likewise. Looking at estimates from geologists on U.S. recoverable reserves, Hubbert estimated the number at two hundred million barrels, and factored the barrels into a bell curve, which put the year of U.S. peak oil at 1971.[104] The idea was rejected until 1970, when U.S. oil production started to decline. Today, the United States imports more than half the oil it uses, whereas in the early 1900s it imported only 10 percent.[105] In 1995, Hubbert's method was applied to world oil production, and many estimates have placed global peak production between 2000 and 2010,[106] with peak global oil discovery having occurred back in 1965.[107]

Just as U.S. peak oil was being realized, oil crises hit. The Organization of the Petroleum Exporting Countries (OPEC), formed in 1960 to allow for greater supplier control over world oil supply, had grown to include twelve nations by 1973. That year, OPEC raised prices, while its Arab member countries declared an oil embargo against the United States in response to the Arab-Israeli War. Another contraction in supply followed the Iranian revolution of 1979. Oil prices soared.

The oil crises of the 1970s had serious effects on the United States by creating massive gas shortages during a decade of "stagflation," simultaneous inflation and reduced economic growth, which many connected to higher gas prices. Throughout the country there were calls for conservation and energy independence, due not only to frustration with oil companies and economic concerns, but also to a growing awareness of environmental problems and anger over ecological disasters. The revelations in Rachel Carson's *Silent Spring* (1962), followed by the large Santa Barbara oil spill and the Cuyahoga River catching fire in 1969, prompted people around the country to mobilize for environmental protections.[108] Activists also drew attention to oil's harmful impacts, including smog from transportation fuels, deforestation and ecosystem destruction from oil exploration and development, and chemical contamination from drilling and refining.[109] By the late 1970s, the United States had adopted fuel efficiency standards for motor vehicles and created government incentives for the use of renewable energy and public transportation.

Despite these moves toward conservation and energy independence, however, a small group of U.S. officials had already ensured the country's continued reliance on oil. In 1974, the Nixon administration negotiated with OPEC countries for the pricing of oil in dollars, helping anchor the floating currency after the 1971 revocation of the gold standard. International meetings also discussed how OPEC's annual earnings—hundreds of billions of dollars throughout the mid- to late 1970s—would be reinvested into the market. Many "petrodollars" were lent to governments of "developing" nations in the interest of modernization, setting off a debt crisis and entangling many of these nations in repayments far greater than their original loans, due to rising interest rates, inflation, and currency devaluations.[110] The U.S. government also secured petrodollars by selling weapons to oil-producing nations,[111] most notably both Iraq and Iran during the Iraq-Iran War, as well as stocks and securities, through which a small group of wealthy Saudis has invested nearly a trillion dollars since the 1970s.[112] In short, both oil and overseas debt created demand for and thus helped stabilize the dollar, with funds recycled back to U.S. interests through debt repayments and the sale of weapons and securities. Even after it had stopped being the world's major source of petroleum, the United States remained heavily dependent on oil for its political, economic, and military power.

While gas prices went up for U.S. consumers through the 1970s, oil companies posted large profits, which led to congressional and Federal Trade Commission (FTC) investigations into the use of price fixing, and questions about the industry's extensive influence on U.S. politics and the economy. The investigation was later called off by President Reagan, who rolled back antitrust regulations altogether, cutting the FTC's budget in half and staffing this agency, too, with free market supporters.[113] Meanwhile, as many countries turned toward conservation and oil demand fell, OPEC countries began competing with each other for market share, helping drive down prices. Soon oil use rebounded. Lower prices contributed to the globalization of oil production, as many large companies found it more economic to outsource manufacturing needs than to produce domestically, leading to a flood of low-cost and disposable consumer goods for the First World. New fuel efficiency standards for automobiles were rejected in the 1980s, and the 1990s heralded the reign of the woefully inefficient sport utility vehicle (SUV), modeled on military combat jeeps and subject to lower fuel standards than cars.[114] With lax regulation, oil companies began merging again, absorbing smaller domestic companies in the 1980s and merging large corporations in the 1990s, such as Chevron and Texaco; BP, Amoco, and Arco; Conoco and Phillips; Shell and Pennzoil; and Exxon and Mobil. By 2001 five corporations—Exxon, BP, Chevron, Phillips-Tosco, and Marathon—controlled 61 percent of the U.S. retail gas market, 47 percent of the U.S. oil refinery market, and 41 percent of U.S. exploration and production.[115]

Oil supply, however, was still uncertain. When dealing with countries that had nationalized production, oil companies had to rely upon marketing and service contracts, since they did not have direct control over the reserves.[116] Nervous about this precarious position, government officials such as former secretary of state Henry Kissinger began talking about taking control over pockets of Middle East oil during the Nixon administration.[117] Although the ideas were not put into action, they continued to develop, particularly among neoconservatives as espoused in the think tank Project for a New American Century (PNAC). Neo-conservatives openly believe in the use of U.S. economic and military force to maintain U.S. hegemony throughout the world. In 1997, PNAC sent President Clinton a letter arguing that the focus of U.S. foreign policy should be removing Iraqi leader Saddam Hussein from power.[118] While Clinton did not fully execute such a policy, soon PNAC members such as Donald Rumsfeld, Paul Wolfowitz, Richard Perle, and Dick Cheney found themselves inside the presidential administration of George W. Bush.

Bush/Cheney marked the first presidential ticket featuring two former oil company presidents; Bush at the time had more experience running an oil company than working in government.[119] Both also had backgrounds in the military-industrial complex. The Bush family's power developed alongside the fossil fuel industry, stretching from Rockefeller to Ken Lay.[120] According to former Republican strategist Kevin Phillips, the Bush family exemplifies the interaction among oil interests, the financial sector, the military-industrial complex, and the intelligence community: family members have close ties to the CIA, domestic and overseas oil production, and banks and other financial institutions like the Carlyle Group, which funds arms operations.[121] Cheney's career also spans government and intelligence as well as oil and the military; he served in both congressional and executive positions, and as CEO and chairman of the private military contracting firm Halliburton. The firm provides services for both oil production and military-related projects, making it a "private sector bridge" between the oil industry and the military-industrial complex.[122]

During the 2000 presidential election, Bush and Cheney received record contributions from the fossil fuel industry, as well as from power companies such as Enron and defense industries such as Halliburton.[123] They entered office with their own mandate, immediately made clear with Cheney's 2001 energy plan calling for the accelerated use of fossil fuels.[124] Peabody and its affiliates had directed $900,000 to the Republican Party during the campaign, and three of its executives were subsequently named to Bush's energy advisory team. The advisory team announced the accelerated use of coal, and Peabody went public in 2001—raising $420 million, much more than analysts had expected before the presidential election.[125] For power companies, the administration refused to cap energy prices as companies such as Enron manipulated energy supplies to gather record profits.[126] For the oil industry, government officials quietly implemented a policy of "royalty relief," neglecting to collect billions owed to taxpayers.[127] Further, they opened up 26 million acres of federal land to oil and gas drilling, denied 220 million acres of wilderness protection, and edited scientific reports to downplay threats to endangered species.[128] The Energy Policy Act of 2005 gave $4.4 billion in subsidies to fossil fuel companies, administered by a private consortium with board members from Halliburton and Marathon Oil.[129] Meanwhile, the Department of the Interior's Minerals Management Services took the phrase "in bed with industry" far too literally, as it was discovered that some government officials were snorting cocaine and having sex with the very oil company representatives they were regulating.[130] This lax regulatory environment surrounded the April 2010 BP rig explosion in the Gulf of Mexico, the largest oil spill in U.S. history.

While ramping up and subsidizing the use of fossil fuels, the Bush administration also quickly focused on a policy of counterterrorism and "democracy building" in the Middle East. The invasions of Afghanistan and Iraq were portrayed as imperative responses to the attacks of September 11, 2001. The multiplying false premises and lies around the Iraq War, however, made it seem much less like an al-Qaeda counteroffensive, and much more like an extension of PNAC's original plans for Iraq. Further, the reinstatement of a previously stalled project for an oil pipeline across Afghanistan raises questions about additional motivations in that country's invasion.[131] Most notably, there were no government calls for attacking Saudi Arabia, where most of the September 11 hijackers originated.

Through this "War on Terror," many within the Bush administration enjoyed lucrative government contracts for affiliated private military companies, such as Halliburton and its subsidiary Kellogg, Brown, and Root (KBR), as private contracts expanded with the 2002 creation of the Department of Homeland Security.[132] Other contractors, like Blackwater (now Xe), acted as a type of privatized military force, exempted from domestic and overseas laws.[133] The invasions also created government-funded contracts for infrastructure construction and repair, and further opened up the countries to transnational business investment, what author Naomi Klein calls "disaster capitalism."[134] In 2008, ExxonMobil, Shell, Total, Chevron, and BP entered final negotiations with Iraq's new oil ministry for no-bid contracts to service Iraq's largest fields,[135] although the deal came under criticism from some U.S. senators and was later withdrawn. Nevertheless, by the end of the Bush administration large oil companies were posting record earnings, and in terms of annual profits, Exxon became the most profitable company in history.[136]

Voted in with overwhelming support from the fossil fuel industry, the George W. Bush administration further increased U.S. structural dependence on coal and oil, with the bulk of the profits flowing to a select group of energy, military, and financial interests, cutting off the potential for such funds to be channeled toward other uses, including alternative modes of power and production. Meanwhile, the effects of climate change were growing increasingly apparent, and the warnings more dire...

THE HISTORY OF THE Inupiaq people is a nomadic, subsistence lifestyle of adaptation and migration with the wildlife, but for decades the people of Kivalina had noticed subtle changes that indicated a warming climate. These included poor ocean ice conditions that changed the way the community hunted on the ocean, and melting permafrost in many areas of Alaska, including the Inupiaq people's aboriginal territory. Other changes included earlier than normal migration of sea mammals—a main staple of the Inupiaq people's diet—and unpredictable weather conditions, among many other small differences. At first the people were able to adapt to such small changes in order to continue to subsist on the wild foods that the land, sea, and air had provided for hundreds of years. Adaptation was the norm for the Inupiaq people and easily accomplished during earlier changes to the Arctic climate. But the changes have been increasing, making adaptation difficult, and our migration ended back in 1905 when the Kivalina school was built.

—KIVALINA TRIBAL ADMINISTRATOR COLLEEN SWAN

FOUR

GLOBAL WHAT?

The growing understanding of anthropogenic warming has been a process of international, cross-disciplinary scientific inquiry and collaboration going back more than a century. Weather refers to atmospheric conditions including temperature, wind, and precipitation over a short period of time, while climate measures the mean (average) and variability of weather over a relatively longer period of time.[1] The term "global warming" describes the increasing average surface temperature of the earth due to steady buildup of heat-trapping gases in our lower atmosphere, while "climate change" more fully captures the scope of the effects.

In the 1820s, the French physicist and mathematician Joseph Fourier hypothesized that, for the earth to have the warm climate that it does, it must retain some of the sun's light rays as heat, what later became known as the "greenhouse effect."[2] The equations and data available at the time were too limited to allow for accurate calculations, but the physics were sufficient to show that the earth was too distant from the sun to be as warm as it is without some intermediary force.[3] In 1859, Royal Society scientist John Tyndall tested the radioactive properties of gases and found water vapor and carbon dioxide were strong absorbers of thermal radiation (heat).[4] Today we know that these so-called greenhouse gases, which also include methane, nitrous oxide, ozone, and aerosols, are transparent to the sun's light rays but trap some of the thermal radiation emitted back from the earth, thereby warming the planet.

In 1896, Swedish electrochemist Svante Arrhenius, doing meticulous numerical calculations that can be seen as a forerunner to climate modeling,[5] argued that halving the atmospheric carbon dioxide would lower Europe's temperature by 4° to 5°C.[6] Drawing upon industrial emission data from his colleague Arvid Högbom, and factoring in calculations of absorption by oceans, Arrhenius then calculated that doubling the carbon dioxide in the atmosphere would raise temperatures by 5° to 6°C, a finding that is remarkably close to many current estimates.[7] Given the much lower scale of industrial emissions at the time, however, these potential consequences were not necessarily a concern.

Government weather services began recording temperature measurements systematically during the nineteenth century, and by the 1930s there were millions of temperature records for stations around the world. Combing through the data led to observations that temperatures had generally increased since the late nineteenth century, and a 1934 U.S. Weather Bureau study verified those observations.[8]

In the 1930s, English engineer Guy Stewart Callendar gathered Northern Hemisphere temperatures dating back to 1900 and also observed a warming trend.[9] He then examined the best available measurements of atmospheric carbon dioxide for the same period and found it had gone up 6 percent.[10] In 1938, Callendar drew upon the scientific literature on thermal radiation and greenhouse gases to present a paper before the British Meteorology Society arguing that humans were warming the planet.[11] Callendar saw this in a positive light, however, thinking it would perhaps prevent the onset of another ice age.[12] Others dismissed Callendar's theory, thinking it unlikely that humans could affect the climate, and that oceans and organic matter would maintain "homeostatic regulation" by absorbing excess carbon dioxide emissions.[13]

World War II and the Cold War sparked the U.S. military's interest in climate, to gain a better understanding of the atmosphere and oceans for military planning.[14] By the end of the 1950s, increased government funding and technological innovation helped create digital computers that enabled far more complicated calculations of atmospheric circulation patterns, eventually producing climate models.[15] Simple climate models use computer algorithms to measure the balance between incoming solar energy and outgoing terrestrial (heat) energy, while more complex models take into account other variables such as temperature, pressure, and winds, breaking up the ocean and atmosphere into a three-dimensional grid and using the underlying physical, chemical, and biological relationships to calculate the properties for each grid box and the interactions between them.

Additional developments in measuring the radioactive isotope carbon-14 ("carbon dating") allowed for the fingerprinting of industrial emissions, as the isotope forms naturally in the atmosphere from cosmic radiation but has usually long since decayed in fossil fuels.[16] The change in the ratio of atmospheric carbon isotopes is known as the Suess effect, based on the observation by physical chemist Hans Suess that the carbon-14 levels of younger tree rings were being diluted by the presence of depleted fossil fuel carbon, suggesting that fossil fuel emissions were accumulating in the atmosphere.

The question was how much of the additional carbon dioxide from fossil fuels was being absorbed by natural "carbon sinks," such as oceans. Carbon dioxide monitoring stations were established around the world, but results were mixed as the stations were subject to interference, or "noise," from local carbon sources. To measure carbon uptake in oceans, Suess collaborated with Robert Revelle at the Scripps Institute of Oceanography. They assessed the declining relative rates of atmospheric carbon-14, as well as carbon-13, in various sea- and land-based life forms (carbon-13 is more abundant in natural, non-plant sources such as volcano emissions, as opposed to the ancient plants and animals constituting fossil fuels). In 1957, Revelle and Suess published that it took about a decade for a typical molecule of atmospheric carbon dioxide to be absorbed by the ocean.[17] Although they went on to question Callendar's analysis that carbon dioxide levels had risen 10 percent due to the burning of industrial fuels, they did note that the surface of the ocean served as a natural "buffer zone," or a chemical resistance to full carbon dioxide absorption. Revelle first noted this effect in 1955 when studying radioactive residues from atomic bomb tests, which tended to spread out in thin sheets over the surface layer rather than dispersing through the ocean.

In 1959, meteorologists Bert Bolin and Erik Eriksson, building upon the research on seawater surface buffering, found that while seawater absorbed atmospheric carbon dioxide quickly—more recent estimates put the rate at five years—most of the absorbed gas evaporated back into the air before it could reach subsurface currents and be circulated away by the oceans.[18] Bolin and Eriksson went on to caution that if industrial emissions continued to rise, the effect on climate might be radical.

Recruited by Revelle and Suess, geochemist Charles David Keeling set out to get an accurate measurement of the concentration of greenhouse gases in the atmosphere. To eliminate the noise of nearby industrial emissions, Keeling took carbon dioxide measurements of pristine air in Antarctica and atop the Mauna Loa volcano in Hawaii. After only

two years of collecting data, Keeling reported in 1960 that the baseline
level of carbon dioxide had measurably risen, at a rate equivalent to what
would be expected if the oceans were absorbing about half the world's
industrial emissions, rather than all of them.[19] Keeling continued taking
measurements, which showed levels slightly lower in the spring, when
carbon dioxide is absorbed, and slightly higher in the fall, when matter
decomposes (what some call "the earth's breath")—yet year after year
sloping ever upward, visually documenting the rising concentration of
carbon dioxide in our atmosphere.[20] The graph, known as Keeling's
curve, is still widely cited by scientists. By the 1960s, biologists and natural scientists had linked up with geochemists and atmospheric scientists to increase understanding of the carbon cycle.

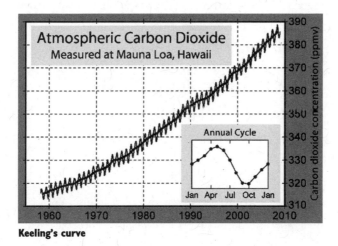

Keeling's curve

Yet the 1960s and '70s, average global temperatures in the Northern Hemisphere remained relatively cool, due to both a weather cycle in
the North Atlantic Ocean winds and the cooling effects of aerosol
emissions from industrial haze, which reflect the sun's rays away from
the earth.[21] Some scientists wondered if past warming had been due to

the "heat island" effect—absorption of heat by smog, black roads, and roofs, usually in urban areas. And some believed the lower temperatures marked the onset of another cooling period, in line with the Milankovitch cycles—periodic shifts in the earth's position relative to the sun, highly correlated to past ice ages—leading a few scientists to argue that the world was headed toward a profound cooling.[22]

In 1975, New Zealand scientists reported that while the Northern Hemisphere had seemed to be cooling, the Southern Hemisphere had been warming, supporting the argument that the cooling had been due to aerosol emissions, which were more pronounced in the north. Ironically, once the north moved to clamp down on aerosol emissions, the warming from greenhouse gases became more apparent.

More evidence of anthropogenic warming was unearthed in the 1980s, as samples of ancient air trapped in ice cores showed correlations between carbon dioxide levels and temperature.[23] A two-kilometer-long ice core drilled in 1985, carrying a 150,000-year record, showed carbon dioxide levels rose and fell in line with records of past temperature shifts.[24] Records going back 800,000 years show carbon dioxide levels got as low as 180 parts per million (ppm) in cold periods and 280 ppm in warm periods, but never higher.[25] In 1980, the concentration of carbon dioxide in the atmosphere was 340 ppm.[26] As of 2011, it is about 390 ppm and rising at an average rate of about 2 ppm a year.

In the United States, a National Aeronautics and Space Administration (NASA) study led by James Hansen factored in oft-neglected Southern Hemisphere temperatures to calculate world average temperatures. In 1981, Hansen's group reported in the journal *Science* that the global average temperature rose 0.2°C between the mid-1960s and 1980, yielding a total warming of 0.4°C in the past century, primarily a result of greenhouse gas emissions.[27] Shortly thereafter a study in Britain agreed with

Hansen's results, and a 1986 study in East Anglia factored in surface temperatures for ocean regions and found considerable warming since the late nineteenth century, with the greatest increase occurring as of the 1970s.[28]

The 1980s proceeded to contain three of the warmest years in the 134-year historical temperature record. In 1988, Hansen testified to the U.S. Congress that he believed with 99 percent confidence that substantial global warming was under way, and would rise significantly unless greenhouse gas emissions were reduced.[29] Hansen was particularly alarmed because the earth is already locked into a certain amount of warming, as carbon dioxide, once emitted, can remain in the atmosphere for over a century.

By 1988, the United Nations and the World Meteorological Organization had created the Intergovernmental Panel on Climate Change (IPCC), a group of about 2,500 international climate scientists who evaluate the research linking anthropogenic greenhouse gases and other emissions to global climate change. IPCC assessments are designed to form a basis for international understanding and action through the UN Framework Convention on Climate Change (UNFCCC). In 1990, IPCC scientists completed their first assessment report for policymakers, stating they were certain human activities were increasing greenhouse gas emissions and warming,[30] with the second report, in 1995, concluding there was a discernible human influence on climate.[31] The groundwork was set for an international treaty to limit greenhouse gas emissions.

Evidence of anthropogenic warming seemed overwhelming. To be sure, not all scientists were fully convinced, with some highlighting gray areas in the data. Many uncertainties have since been accounted for, however, and those remaining involve complexities of detail that do not discount the overwhelming scientific consensus concerning anthropogenic warming.[32] For example, early measurements of satellite data originally showed little measurable warming. The data was later determined to have been affected by the influence of stratospheric cooling (the stratosphere is the layer beyond the lower atmosphere), caused by ozone depletion due to chlorofluorocarbons (CFCs), and showed warming once that factor had been accounted for.[33] Another area of uncertainty concerned inconclusive balloon measurements, which were found not to have registered warming initially due to the heating of the instrument in the daylight.[34] Some scientists question the efficacy and reliability of climate change models,[35] although the models have proved remarkably accurate in many simulations of past and present conditions, are improving as new observations are fed in, and are not the only source of data on anthropogenic climate change.[36] Skeptics have argued that past temperature records are unreliable due to the urban "heat island" effect, as built-up areas often retain more heat than rural areas, but numerous studies have found any urban-related warming trends to be on an order of magnitude lower than overall warming, measured per decade.[37] Finally, some have pointed to the role of sunspots, or solar variability, in warming. The IPCC notes such variability can account for only a tiny fraction of the heightened warming since the Industrial Revolution,[38] and a 2007 Royal Society study by solar physicists found that solar variability, despite its historical effect on climate, could not account for the spike in warming since 1985. Others note that if warming were caused by the sun, it would heat the whole atmosphere, whereas warming is taking place in the lower atmosphere, consistent with the effect of greenhouse gases that prevent the heat from flowing upward.[39]

The science was reaching top U.S. officials. Revelle and Keeling, among others, authored a report on the increase in carbon dioxide emissions and the possible dire effects as part of the Johnson administration's

1965 report, *Restoring the Quality of Our Environment*. President Nixon's Democratic adviser, Daniel Patrick Moynihan, wrote in a 1969 memo that it was "pretty clearly agreed" that carbon dioxide levels were rising fast and would increase the average temperature near the earth's surface, and that such dangers justified government action.[40]

As climate change research strengthened and the evidence grew increasingly alarming, a confluence of the fossil fuel industry, the PDI, and supportive politicians came together in their common goal of preventing regulatory action on global warming. In 1983, a committee of the U.S. National Academy of Sciences chaired by physicist William Nierenberg reframed the growing consensus around anthropogenic warming as a "nonproblem" that would have limited effects humans could adapt to, as with past changes in human history. Nierenberg was cofounder of the George C. Marshall Institute, whose stated purpose was to "raise the level of scientific literacy of the American people in fields of science with an impact on national security and other areas of public concern."[41] In 1989, James Hansen's testimony to Congress was edited by president George H. W. Bush's Office of Management and Budget to emphasize uncertainties.[42]

The coal industry also responded to Hansen's 1988 congressional testimony, primarily through the Western Fuels Association (WFA), headed by Fred Palmer, who later became vice president of Peabody. As outlined in Ross Gelbspan's *The Heat Is On*, the WFA actively sought to refute the growing consensus on climate change, stating in its report that "when [the climate change] controversy first erupted at the peak of summer in 1988, Western Fuels Association decided it was important to take a stand.... [S]cientists were found who are skeptical about the potential for climate change. Among them were [Pat] Michaels and S. Fred Singer of the University of Virginia."[43] The report added that WFA had approached Pat Michaels about serving as editor of a quarterly publication on climate change, *World Climate Review*, which WFA agreed to finance.[44]

While there are scientists who have raised important questions around climate change science, pointing to areas in need of further research and thus pushing fuller understanding, this is not the mold of scientists like Singer and Michaels. The former could accurately be called skeptics, reserving judgment on the merits of research until data has proved consistent, replicable, and reliable. Michaels and particularly Singer, however, point to uncertainties not to push for and increase understanding, but to delay and muddy it. They also have so many crossovers with the PDI that they would be more accurately described as public relations agents.

Singer is a physicist who, prior to questioning global warming science, also questioned the harms of environmental tobacco smoke and ozone depletion. He admitted (and later recanted) that he had received funding from fossil fuel companies and, in 1995, actively solicited an oil industry public relations outlet for money to host a series of panels, lectures, and publications to publicly counter the IPCC findings.[45] Michaels fought for less stringent regulations on ozone depletion, and has received hundreds of thousands of dollars in funding from the WFA, the Edison Electric Institute, and the German Coal Mining Association to publicize his view that global warming will have minor effects that may be beneficial.[46] Singer has cited false or nonexistent data to back up his contrarian views,[47] publicized studies after they had been proven inaccurate,[48] and, along with Michaels, disingenuously attacked climate change science and scientists while downplaying the magnitude of consensus on anthropogenic warming.[49] Both have published articles, books, and research in their own journals and websites, and have

even testified before Congress, invited by fellow climate change contrarians.[50] Their efforts have been aided by U.S. media outlets that
equate objectivity and balance with merely presenting different sides of
an issue, even when one side is widespread scientific consensus and the
other is a handful of industry-funded contrarians, leading to measurable increases in U.S. public uncertainty.[51]

In 1990, Singer founded the Science and Environmental Policy
Project (SEPP), an organization "skeptical" of global warming and
ozone depletion, headed by former National Academy of Sciences
(NAS) president Frederick Seitz. In 1995, Singer created the Leipzig
Declaration, allegedly signed by scientists who questioned anthropogenic warming, but later shown to have many signatories who were
not scientists or who claimed to have not actually signed the declaration.[52] In 1998, Seitz put together and circulated the now widely
mocked "Oregon Petition," designed to look like a NAS document
listing scientists skeptical of warming. Those scientists apparently included television character Perry Mason, actor Michael J. Fox, and
Geraldine Halliwell from the pop band Spice Girls, all of whom were
listed among the many other dubious or false signatures on the petition, which was not in fact from NAS. One scientist who did sign was
Seitz, leading NAS to publicly disassociate itself from Seitz's stance.[53]
Before being debunked, however, the petitions were widely circulated
throughout the U.S. media and cited by political representatives to
support inaction on regulating greenhouse gas emissions, particularly
with regard to ongoing UN negotiations.

Shortly after the IPCC was formed in 1989, various industries created the lobbying group Global Climate Coalition, with the stated purpose of "cast[ing] doubt on the theory of global warming."[54] Its early
members included Amoco, the American Forest & Paper Association,

the American Petroleum Institute, Chevron, Chrysler, Cyprus AMAX Minerals, Exxon, Ford, General Motors, Shell Oil, Texaco, and the U.S. Chamber of Commerce, although the coalition eventually came to be dominated by Exxon. The Global Climate Coalition spent $60 million in political donations and millions more on propaganda promoting scientific doubt,[55] as well as cost-benefit analyses suggesting regulation would cause widespread unemployment and inflation.[56] The group went so far as to fund a climate report that measured only three weather stations to suggest global temperatures were not on the rise.[57]

Most notably, the Global Climate Coalition, along with Donald Pearlman's Climate Council, played a prominent role in the international UNFCCC negotiations—the 1992 Rio Earth Summit and the Kyoto talks of 1997. Pearlman works for the U.S. law firm Patton, Boggs & Blow, whose clients include DuPont, Texaco, Exxon, and Shell. He invented a nongovernmental organization, the Climate Council, to gain entry to the UNFCCC negotiations, giving him access to U.S. briefings on the UN proceedings while simultaneously serving as a paid consultant to OPEC representatives for Kuwait and Saudi Arabia.[58] Global Climate Coalition executive director John Schlaes and Pearlman were reported to have drafted a number of U.S.-Saudi amendments designed to stall negotiations.[59] Both the Global Climate Coalition and Pearlman rejected the negotiations' call for binding emission cuts on developed nations and flexibility for developing nations, an approach designed to deal with historic inequities in greenhouse gas emissions.[60] Instead, they argued, developed nations should not accept any binding greenhouse gas reductions unless developing nations are subject to the same cuts, a stance also taken by OPEC nations. Although this argument was ultimately rejected and the U.S. representative agreed to the Kyoto accord, the resolution was never ratified within the United

States. Instead, the Senate passed the Byrd-Hagel resolution, which stated that it was not the sense of the Senate that the United States should be a signatory to Kyoto given its unequal treatment of nations, a stance reflecting the views of the Global Climate Coalition and Donald Pearlman, and eventually adopted by President Clinton and later the George W. Bush administration.

Sociologists Aaron McCright and Riley Dunlap have tracked how industry representatives worked to transform growing national understanding and concern over warming into a "nonproblem," creating a political climate conducive toward rejecting the Kyoto accord.[61] After Kyoto, among U.S. Republicans the public perception of global warming as a problem shrank, marking the beginning of a growing partisan divide concerning climate change and the need for action.[62] The PDI tactics of doubt and uncertainty were also picked up in other countries such as Australia, which like the United States also retains vast supplies of coal.[63] Later, a Freedom of Information Act request unearthed 2001 U.S. State Department documents to the Global Climate Coalition suggesting Bush's decision to pull out of Kyoto had been shaped by the coalition, Pearlman, and Exxon. As reported in the *Guardian* (UK), the document is addressed to the Global Climate Coalition and states that the president "rejected Kyoto, in part, based on input from you," and that undersecretary Paula J. Dobriansky should "solicit GCC [Global Climate Coalition] ideas in alternative to Kyoto as part of continuing dialogue with friends and allies."[64]

Fossil fuel and related industries were aided in their efforts by Philip Morris. As discussed, internal Philip Morris documents obtained through state Medicare settlements detail how, as the EPA moved to regulate secondhand smoke, The Advancement of Sound Science Coalition (TASSC) was created by Philip Morris in 1993 to appear to be a grassroots citizens group fighting government overregulation and "junk science."[65] To give TASSC the appearance of being independent, Philip Morris's public relations firm, APCO, suggested TASSC adopt other issues and solicit a broad range of contributors so that its focus was not solely tobacco, and specifically mentioned global warming as a potential issue to adopt.[66] TASSC created the website www.junkscience.com, which attacked advances in climate change science and popularized the views of climate change contrarians.

Another smoking gun document emerged in a memo leaked from the National Environmental Trust to the *New York Times* in 1998. The memo detailed that a dozen people working for big oil companies, trade associations, and conservative think tanks had been meeting at the American Petroleum Institute's Washington headquarters to propose a $5 million campaign to convince the public that global warming science was riddled with controversy and uncertainty, mentioning climate contrarian Fred Singer's SEPP, the George C. Marshall Institute, and TASSC as potential sounding boards for their message.[67] The plan was to train up to twenty "respected climate scientists" on media and public outreach with the aim of "raising questions about and undercutting the 'prevailing scientific wisdom,'" particularly "the Kyoto treaty's scientific underpinnings," so that elected officials "will seek to prevent progress toward implementation."[68] Those involved confirmed the authenticity of the draft documents, but argued the plans had not been formally approved and were meant to offer a "sound science alternative" to the IPCC.[69]

Outraged, Greenpeace began documenting the efforts of climate change deniers, publishing its research at www.exxonsecrets.org, named as such due to Exxon's prominent role in funding organizations skeptical of warming. According to the site, since 1998 Exxon has donated over $22 million dollars to nearly fifty policy groups and think tanks skeptical of warming, including TASSC, SEPP, and the George C. Marshall Institute, while simultaneously divesting itself of alternative energy holdings. The site's interactive map and a report by the Union of Concerned Scientists show that many of the think tanks and organizations have overlapping collections of spokespeople serving as staff, board members, and scientific advisors.[70] Recently, Exxon has been outspent in funding climate skeptic organizations by Koch Industries, a large private company involved in refining and trading fossil fuels, including tar sands—and, as mentioned, the sponsor of the corporate rights meetings attended by Justices Scalia and Thomas.[71]

No doubt one of the most profitable investments of the fossil fuel industry, however, was the presidential campaign of George W. Bush. Upon taking office in 2001, the Bush administration immediately announced that the United States was pulling out of the Kyoto negotiations. To support this position, the administration moved to block the governmental publication of any information on global warming. In 2003, the Competitive Enterprise Institute, heavily funded by Exxon, invoked the Data Quality Act to challenge the release of an interagency government report on climate change, known as the National Assessment, arguing that it was based on faulty computer models. Giving the appearance of deferring to the charges, the administration "agreed" to release the study with the caveat that the report state it had not been subject to Data Quality Act guidelines.[72] Email exchanges between the White House and the Competitive Enterprise Institute later suggested the Bush administration was actively working with the institute to suppress and discredit such government scientific reports on climate change.[73] When the EPA published a report in 2003 with six paragraphs on climate change, the White House deleted five of them, and instructed the EPA to insert instead a reference to a study disputing the global warming "hypothesis," written by scientists associated with an Exxon-funded think tank.[74]

Congressional members also did their part. As the McCain-Lieberman bill to reduce carbon emissions gathered momentum in the Senate in 2003, the chairman of the Committee on Environment and Public Works, Republican James Inhofe of Oklahoma—who has received more than a million dollars in campaign contributions from the energy and coal sector since taking office[75]—took to the Senate floor and delivered a two-hour speech against the science on climate change. Citing Fred Singer as a source for his skepticism, Inhofe concluded by asking if global warming was "the greatest hoax ever perpetrated on the American people."[76] After the speech he received an award for "rational, science-based thinking and policy" from the Annapolis Center for Science-Based Public Policy, an association heavily financed by oil and utility companies.[77]

The administration then went on to silence government scientists, telling NASA personnel they could not speak publicly about new data on ozone and air pollution until the 2004 election, and threatening NASA scientist James Hansen with "dire consequences" if he continued calling for a reduction in greenhouse gas emissions.[78] Meteorologists were told to check with the administration before they talked to the press, to ensure they did not suggest climate change was affecting weather, particularly hurricanes.[79] And many government scientists reported that the administration tampered with and edited their reports.[80] The suppression grew so stifling that the Union of Concerned Scientists published a fifty-page report detailing Bush administration tampering, based on responses to a questionnaire sent to more than 1,600 climate scientists at seven federal agencies.[81]

In June 2005, it was found that a federal report on climate change had been edited by Philip Cooney, chief of staff for the White House Council on Environmental Quality, to cast climate science as uncertain. Prior to working in the White House, Cooney had served as a lobbyist for the American Petroleum Institute, the largest oil lobby in Washington, D.C.,[82] where the meetings to discuss the fossil fuel industry's planned misinformation campaign had taken place. After news grew of Cooney's edits, he resigned and went to work for ExxonMobil.

In 2005, Bush acknowledged anthropogenic warming, but did not propose to do anything about it. Instead, the administration avoided the EPA's 2007 report on climate change by claiming they had not opened the email attachment, an excuse so pathetic it encapsulates their utter disdain toward the issue. During the Bush administration's eight years of inaction, temperatures continued to climb, most of the world's glaciers were in retreat, and melting Arctic permafrost was steadily releasing methane into the atmosphere, regarded as a potential catalyst to runaway warming.[83] Climate change also contributes to severe weather events, with warm air absorbing more water vapor, increasing precipitation that can manifest as flooding and large snowstorms, and sucking up moisture in already dry areas, aggravating evaporation and droughts, while rising sea temperatures help create conditions that can fuel stronger hurricanes.[84]

In 2009, an internal Global Climate Coalition document was leaked to the New York Times: a primer written in 1995 for coalition members by an industry-hired advisory committee on climate science, admitting that the "scientific basis for the greenhouse effect and the potential impact of human emissions of greenhouse gases such as carbon dioxide on climate is well established and cannot be denied."[85] The committee also wrote that "contrarian theories raise interesting questions about our total understanding of climate processes, but they do not offer convincing arguments against the conventional model of greenhouse gas emission-induced climate changes," a statement the Global Climate Coalition's operating committee voted to remove from the primer before its distribution to members.[86] The document shows that the Global Climate Coalition operating committee knew the arguments of climate change contrarians were weak but continued to publish them as "proof" against the existence of warming, and its members knew anthropogenic warming could not be denied but continued to do so.

Powerful interests opposing action on climate change have so far been just as influential in the courtroom as they have in the political and executive branches. Each of the three federal public nuisance claims filed as of 2007 against fossil fuel or related industries were initially dismissed partly or wholly on the grounds that global warming was a "political question" not suitable for the judicial branch and best left to the political branches (executive and legislative), even as both those branches refused to act on global warming.

The EPA itself refused to act. In 1999, multiple organizations petitioned the EPA to regulate greenhouse gas emissions from new motor vehicles under the Clean Air Act, a request the EPA denied in 2003.[87] In denying the petition, the EPA argued that Congress had not given the agency such authority, and that, remarkably, "President Bush has established a comprehensive global climate change policy."[88] Further, the EPA argued, "The international nature of climate change also has implications for foreign policy, which the President directs,"[89] referring to Kyoto. Petitioners challenged the EPA's decision, and in 2005 the Court of Appeals for the District of Columbia, in a 2 to 1 decision, upheld the EPA's argument, agreeing that regulating carbon dioxide had policy implications that could interfere with U.S. efforts to reduce greenhouse gas emissions from other countries, thus allowing the EPA to deny the petitions.[90]

A full court rejected the request by states and environmental groups to reconsider the ruling, eventually landing the case in the Supreme Court. In 2007, the Supreme Court directed the EPA to either regulate carbon dioxide emissions or offer a compelling reason not to do so.[91] Until the Supreme Court ruling, however, the EPA had interpreted the lack of congressional and executive action on greenhouse gas emissions as a "comprehensive" policy, intended to leverage the U.S. position in international climate change negotiations that Bush refused to take part in, and courts had upheld the rationale as legally sound.

The impartiality of the judges in the initial EPA cases should be questioned, however, as two of the judges involved in the rulings had attended a judicial seminar hosted by the Foundation for Research on the Environment and Economics (FREE), an antiregulation organization heavily funded by corporations such as Exxon and conservative foundations such as Coors. In 2002, FREE hosted a five-day judicial seminar entitled "Understanding the Ecology, Economics, and Effects of Climate Change." The federal judges at this particular conference were warned about "deep scientific uncertainties" concerning global warming and the problems with "regulation by litigation."[92] Two of the Washington, D.C., circuit judges in attendance, David Sentelle and Douglas Ginsburg, were key in supporting the EPA's inaction. Sentelle acted as the deciding vote upholding the EPA's refusal to regulate, and he and Ginsburg were part of the 4 to 3 majority rejecting the motion for reconsideration.

As the EPA resisted action, three federal public nuisance lawsuits were filed, asserting the rights of individuals and states to have climate change addressed in the courts. While the lawsuits argued that their suits fit the definition of common law, the three claims filed between 2005 and 2007—*Connecticut v. American Electric Power Company, Cal-*

ifornia v. General Motors, and *Comer v. Murphy*—were each initially dismissed partly or wholly as a "political question" inappropriate for the courts, or nonjusticiable.

The political question doctrine goes back to an 1849 Supreme Court case, *Luther v. Borden*, in which the court declined ruling on the legitimacy of a democratically elected, grassroots "People's Government" of Rhode Island, saying the matter was a question for the political branches, not the courts.[93] Since the *Luther* ruling, courts gradually adopted six separate formulations for determining if a case constitutes a political question, laid out in the 1926 Supreme Court case *Baker v. Carr*: 1) a textually demonstrable commitment of the issue to a coordinate political department; 2) a lack of judicially discoverable and manageable standards for resolving it; 3) the impossibility of deciding without an initial policy determination of a kind clearly for nonjudicial discretion; 4) the impossibility of the court's undertaking independent resolution without expressing lack of respect due coordinate branches of the government; 5) an unusual need for unquestioning adherence to a political decision already made; 6) the potentiality of embarrassment from multifarious pronouncements by various departments on one question.[94] The Supreme Court went on to state that unless "one of these formulations is inextricable from the case at bar, there should be no dismissal for non-justiciability on the ground of a political question's presence."[95] Since *Baker*, the Supreme Court has ruled only two cases a political question. In considering public nuisance global warming cases, however, federal courts have adopted the doctrine quite liberally.

In 2005, eleven states, the City of New York, and private land trusts sought to cap carbon dioxide emissions from five major electric utilities in *Connecticut v. American Electric Power Co.* In the claim, the plaintiffs argued carbon dioxide emissions from coal-fired power plants constitute a public nuisance under both federal and state law, and defendants have practical, feasible, and economically viable options for reducing emissions without significant increases to electricity costs. Defendant companies moved to dismiss the claim on multiple grounds, particularly preemption, arguing the lawsuit should be barred by federal regulations like the Clean Air Act, even though the EPA was refusing to regulate carbon dioxide emissions.[96] Rather than address preemption, however, Judge Loretta Preska for the Southern District Court of New York instead dismissed the claim as a "political question" best left to the executive and legislative branches.

Invoking the political question doctrine, Judge Preska argued that "Congress and the Executive Branch have taken several steps to better understand and address the complex issue of global warming."[97] The several steps listed, however, were a series of congressional requests for further information on climate change, ending with Bush's withdrawal from Kyoto "because it exempts developing nations who are major emitters, fails to address two major pollutants, and would have a negative economic impact on the United States...which the EPA describes as 'prudent.'"[98] These "actions," Judge Preska argued, constituted a political policy, and any decision by the court would interfere with such policy. She went on to chastise the plaintiffs for the "transcendently legislative nature of this litigation," ignoring the duty of attorneys general to ensure public health.[99]

In October 2006, the State of California filed a similar lawsuit, *California v. General Motors, et al.*, seeking damages from six automobile manufacturers on grounds that greenhouse gas emissions from their vehicles constituted a public nuisance. Before the state court issued a ruling, the Supreme Court determined that greenhouse gas emissions qualify as "pollutants" under the Clean Air Act, authorizing the EPA to regulate.[100] In spite of the Supreme Court decision rejecting the EPA's refusal to regulate carbon dioxide emissions, in 2007 Judge Martin Jenkins of the Northern District Court for California drew upon the EPA's original reasoning, arguing a judicial decision on damages would "potentially undermine the political branches' strategic choices by 'weaken[ing] U.S. efforts to persuade key developing countries to reduce the [greenhouse gas] intensity of their economies.'"[101] Judge Jenkins, like Judge Preska in *AEP*, proceeded to dismiss the claim as a political question.

In August 2007, Judge Louis Guirola for the U.S. District Court for the Southern District of Mississippi wrote a two-page brief against a class action public nuisance lawsuit brought by Gulf Coast residents alleging greenhouse gas emissions from petrochemical companies increased the damages caused by Hurricane Katrina. In an oral ruling for the lawsuit, *Comer v. Murphy Oil Co.*, Judge Guirola dismissed the plaintiffs' claims on both political question and legal standing grounds, arguing the harm could not be traced to individual defendants.[102] Both the *AEP* and *Murphy Oil* decisions have been appealed. *GM* was also appealed, but California voluntarily dropped the claim when a rise in national fuel efficiency standards was announced after Barack Obama assumed office.

In short, the rationale of the fossil fuel industry, the PDI, and conservative government officials—namely that the United States should withhold action on global warming until developing nations are also subject to binding regulations—permeated the legislative branch via the Byrd-Hagel resolution, the Clinton and in particular the Bush administrations, the EPA, and even the district courts and D.C. Court of Appeals, bolstered by the deliberate seeding of doubt on climate change science. The argument about binding emissions for developing nations might hold more weight if so many of its main proponents were not in favor of exporting fossil fuels to these nations and setting up increased manufacturing within their borders, making the argument appear to be less a legitimate call for regulation than a stalling technique that has been far too effective for too long. Reframing this U.S. inaction on climate change as political action, the district courts in the federal public nuisance cases dismissed claims against defendant companies, shutting off one of the few avenues available for the public to hold powerful corporate and government officials accountable for their refusal to acknowledge and act on climate change.

The result? In a 2009 interview, energy secretary Stephen Chu flatly stated that the world will most certainly pass the carbon dioxide tipping points warned of by scientists, a situation in which positive feedbacks could potentially create runaway warming beyond our control.[103] And Chu was referring to the conservative estimate of 450 ppm, which some scientists believe is already too high for a stable climate. We are in for a potentially bumpy ride, one for which many in the United States are totally unprepared, given the levels of misinformation and doubt. Although the pace of climate change research and the understanding of climate change itself have been slow and piecemeal, it was unnecessary for the science to be ridiculed and sabotaged with misinformation. Members of the fossil fuel industry, the PDI, and the U.S. government worked to prevent widespread understanding of climate change, constructing uncertainty and ignorance,[104] deconstructing knowledge,[105] and transforming global warming from a looming threat to a nonproblem,[106] toying with the fate of the entire planet.

Within this political vacuum of action on climate change, the tiny Alaskan village of Kivalina, eroding into the sea, sued fossil fuel companies for damaging their homeland and lying about it—the tip of a much larger and growing climate justice movement.

DUE TO THE LACK of ice formation along the shores of Kivalina, by October 2004 the land began failing. What had once been a normal occurrence of annual fall sea storms became a life-threatening event. As the stormy days progressed, the people became concerned over the amount of land falling into the ocean. The island seemed to be falling apart and disappearing into the Chukchi Sea before the very eyes of its inhabitants. Volunteers from the village began to work feverishly to hold the island together but every effort, every object placed along the edges, was being sucked into the angry sea. The volunteers worked through the pitch darkness of the cold fall night above the Arctic Circle trying to save the people of Kivalina and the island. Evacuation by air was not an option because of the weather conditions and because the village was surrounded by the rough waters of the sea storm. This meant evacuation was also not an option by boat to the mainland. There was nowhere to go and nothing the volunteers did worked to keep the island together—the people were trapped!

—KIVALINA TRIBAL ADMINISTRATOR COLLEEN SWAN

FIVE

THE HUMAN FACE OF GLOBAL WARMING

Kivalina residents on a mound of dirt used for beach nourishment, Kivalina, Alaska, 2008

The Native Village of Kivalina lies approximately 120 miles north of the Arctic Circle, on the tip of a thin, eight-mile-long barrier reef island. The population of about four hundred is primarily Inupiat, with ancestry to the area going back thousands of years to some of the first settlements in the Americas. The Inupiat have been able to survive in the harsh Arctic region through an understanding of and close connection to the cycles and rhythms of the land, with the Inupiaq words for the different seasons translating into their hunting and gathering cycles. This understanding permeates their culture—that is, their daily life—and their ability to live off the land, sustaining themselves and their community, is a source of pride and values. Like many Alaska Native villages, Kivalina has retained a largely subsistence lifestyle.

Aerial view of Kivalina, Alaska, 2008

Kivalina residents report first noting erosion of the island in the 1950s, and in 1992 the community voted to relocate, selecting a new site by 1998. As they tried to engineer the move, however, they found that a government body to assist communities with relocation does not exist. According to city administrator Janet Mitchell, "We talked to everyone we could. But the word *relocation* does not exist at the federal level, and I doubt it exists at the state level." Tribal administrator Colleen Swan reported a similar experience: "There wasn't anyone we could talk to about global warming and what it was doing to our environment. There's no agency in the federal government that deals with climate change." Residents also received little relocation help from their representative tribal corporation, the Northwest Arctic Native Association (NANA), created by the 1971 Alaska Native Claims Settlement Act and seemingly more focused on economic growth than tribal assistance. Caught within gray areas of U.S. and tribal political representation, Kivalina has been struggling to relocate for almost two decades with little success, as climate change comes more quickly and severely, putting the entire village in danger.

Aerial view of Kivalina school and barge, 2008

The erosion of Kivalina and the difficulty facing its residents as they try to relocate raises issues of climate justice, as the people of Kivalina have lived a relatively low-energy, subsistence lifestyle for millennia, yet are facing some of the biggest impacts from climate change. Climate justice is an extension of civil rights and environmental justice movements, which acknowledge that risks to public well-being are unequal, reflecting broader social inequality.[1] Historic discrimination, uneven political representation, and economic inequality have concentrated many working-class and communities of color in more hazardous areas with fewer resources to minimize harms, as is the case with the people of Kivalina.[2]

Alaska, the Aleut word for "great land," is believed to have been the gateway to some of the first human migrations to the Americas, during a glacial period fifteen to thirty thousand years ago. Evidence for this theory was greatly aided by geologist David M. Hopkins who, when sent by the U.S. government to Alaska in the 1940s to seek out suitable locations for military bases, soon turned his research toward the mysteries surrounding the first human migrations to the area. Drawing together an international, multidisciplinary team of experts, including Inupiat with their traditional knowledge, Hopkins helped piece together a sixty-million-year timeline for the submerged land connecting Siberia and Alaska, a mass so large it is called not a bridge but a subcontinent, Beringia. Various fossil records, tree ring dating, and geological records suggest that during the last glaciation, ice sheets locked up the sea, lowering sea levels and exposing the underlying continental shelf, making animal and human passage possible.[3] When the ice sheets melted twelve thousand years ago, the shelf was again inundated, separating the continents and creating the Bering Strait.[4]

The dates of the first indigenous settlements within Alaska are a contested issue. There is evidence of hunting tools going back eleven thousand years, but it is believed settlement occurred even earlier.[5] The term *Eskimo* to refer to Native Arctic people has been rejected by many as pejorative given controversy around its original meaning, which some say is "eaters of raw meat," although this is disputed. Instead, *Inuit* refers to all the indigenous populations inhabiting the Arctic, and *Alaska Natives* refers to the indigenous groups within the state. Alaska's 365 million acres contain more than 200 native villages, many far from urban areas and near the coast or rivers for easier access in hunting, fishing, and gathering wild plants for food. Subsistence activities are still widely practiced and embody the main values of Alaska Native culture: cooperation and respect for the land, which have helped Alaska Natives survive harsh Arctic conditions for thousands of years.[6]

The first European contact with Alaska Natives occurred in 1741, when Danish-born navigator Vitus Bering led the Russian Navy on an exploration of the boundaries of European settlement in the area. After the explorers returned with furs, other Russians soon traveled to Alaska along the Aleutian Islands to expand commercial trading. In the process, native Aleuts were subjugated for labor and trapping, and in thirty years their population decreased from twelve thousand to less than two thousand due to hard labor and disease.[7] Other Alaska Natives also died from disease or were forcibly relocated by subsequent British, French, Spanish, and U.S. travelers,[8] although in some more positive cases business and friendship ties were forged. Despite expanding its influence over the area, Russia never fully established Alaska as a colony and, to relieve its war debt, "sold" Alaska to the United States in 1867 for $7.2 million, at two cents an acre.[9] Alaska Natives were not consulted in the deal, and their legal status and land claims were folded into the ambiguities surrounding Native American rights in general. According to the Treaty of Cession: "The uncivilized tribes [of Alaska] will be subject to such laws and regulations as the United States may, from time to time, adopt in regard to aboriginal tribes of that country."[10]

In 1884, the U.S. government passed the Organic Act, making Alaska a judicial and civil district with limited government officials appointed by the federal government. During this time, the number of American settlers only reached into the hundreds, with much of the country wondering why Congress had bought an "ice box."[11] That changed in the 1890s with the discovery of gold, bringing thousands of miners and settlers and spurring industries in fishing, trapping, mining, and mineral production—as well as calls from the new arrivals for more local government. The efforts toward local governance were opposed by wealthy businessmen such as J. P. Morgan and Simon Guggenheim, who wanted to retain their tight control over several mines, steamships, and railroad companies.[12] In 1911, however, oil wells were struck, and Congress promptly made Alaska a U.S. territory with an elected legislature, although the federal government retained control over the natural resources.

In 1924, Native Americans were granted U.S. citizenship, and the federal government considered it a national duty to "civilize" them,[13] including Alaska Natives. Education was seen as an important force in this mission, and teachers were sent to native settlements to encourage changes in culture, religion, and language. School was taught in English, churches were constructed, and monogamous marriages and patriarchal households were encouraged or enforced, breaking up communal households.[14] Historically nomadic Alaska Natives began settling around the schools and churches, often by order of the U.S. government, which in turn provided small-scale infrastructure and health clinics.[15] What is now the village of Kivalina, for example, had originally been used only as a hunting ground during certain times of the year, but its intermittent inhabitants were ordered to settle permanently on the island and enroll their children in school or face imprisonment. The U.S. Bureau of Indian Affairs was delegated responsibility for Alaska Native programs in 1931, and Congress extended the federal Indian Reorganization Act (IRA) to Alaska in 1936, transforming some villages into federally recognized tribes. Villages were also organized as local governments of Alaska, with jurisdiction over native residents but not the land.[16]

In line with post–World War II modernization, Alaska Natives were instructed to replace their traditional ways with a cash economy.[17] There were few opportunities for wage labor, however, which helped Alaska Natives maintain their largely subsistence lifestyle.[18] Thus many native villages became a mix of modernity and tradition, weaving together U.S., Christian, and ancestral traditions, and blending telephones, TVs, and small motorized vehicles with their subsistence ways.[19] These changes also created tension within communities, between those wanting to be more tightly integrated into the U.S. economy, and those wanting to retain their traditional culture.[20]

During World War II, federally funded military bases were constructed throughout Alaska, contributing to the population growth of some Alaskan cities. Military funding continued after the war, as the area was considered an important strategic location in the Cold War,[21] as well as a potential source of much oil. The U.S. Navy began exploring for petroleum in 1946; oil was found in 1957 on the Kenai Peninsula on the southern coast, with the first well a successful strike that produced nine hundred barrels a day: the first major commercial oil discovery in Alaska.[22] One year later, Alaska statehood was approved, and on January 3, 1959, Alaska officially became the fiftieth state of the union.

Immediately after statehood was proclaimed, Alaska Natives clashed with the federal government over both hunting rights and the proposed testing of nuclear weapons near native villages, bringing to the surface unresolved issues surrounding Alaska Native land rights.[23] Filing numerous land rights claims, Alaska Natives across the state began organizing as the Alaskan Federation of Natives (AFN), seeking sovereignty. Despite the pressure, the issues were left unresolved, even as the State of Alaska staked out federal land claims to lease for oil and gas development, claims overlapping with those of Alaska Natives.[24] In 1966, secretary of the interior Stewart Udall, sympathetic to the native land claims, issued a freeze on all oil and gas leases in the state.[25] Shortly afterward, the largest oilfield in North America was found on Alaska's North Slope—across land Alaska Natives had claimed as their own— and the State of Alaska petitioned to lease the land to oil and gas developers.[26] Both government and oil company officials were eager to drill and construct a Trans-Alaska Pipeline to increase domestic supply, creating a large incentive to quickly settle the land claims issue.[27]

Several government proposals were made, offering little land to Alaska Natives, and were quickly rejected.[28] This helped engender support for an AFN-congressional compromise granting land titles on the condition that the land be transferred not to tribes but to newly created "tribal corporations," chartered under Alaska state corporate law.[29] While this proposal appealed to those Alaska Natives who wanted land rights, it was regarded with suspicion by many others, who disliked the idea of transforming their cultural relations into a corporate structure, and saw the proposal as confusing and ambiguous, with potentially negative implications.[30] The AFN, however, believed the native-run corporations were a chance at economic development and indigenous independence,[31] and together the AFN and the U.S. government agreed to the 1971 Alaska Native Claims Settlement Act (ANCSA).

The act extinguished almost all existing Alaska Native claims to land, and by extension aboriginal hunting and fishing rights, in exchange for titles to one-ninth of the state's land. While one-ninth of the large state is a lot of land, it was far less than Alaska Natives had claimed, and included none of the recently identified oil-rich lands and pipeline territory, despite established native settlements in those areas.[32] As compensation, the act also offered $962.5 million dollars to Alaska Natives. To ensure economic development, the ANCSA created twelve (later thirteen) Alaska Native regional corporations and more than two hundred local village corporations. Local villages held surface rights to their land, while regional corporations held subsurface and mineral rights titles. Regional corporations had final authority over village development plans, and were required to pay out a percentage of the benefits from their economic activities to their native shareholders.[33] Individuals with at least one-quarter native ancestry were allotted shares of stock in their regional corporation and associated village corporation.[34] Over time amendments and legal battles were necessary to address the many issues that arose with the ANCSA, such as allowing for the extension of shares to those born after the act was passed, and the granting of greater legal protections for subsistence hunting and fishing.[35]

After the ANCSA, construction quickly began on the pipeline. Alaska has subsequently become a major source of oil: for the past two decades, more than 80 percent of the state's revenues have derived from petroleum extraction. With oil dominating Alaska's industry, state politicians have become reliant on its revenues, allowing oil companies to exercise even more power within the state government. Oil companies helped defeat state attempts to make the Trans-Alaska Pipeline a public resource[36] and watered down safety regulations on the pipeline and oil shipping,[37] creating the lax and chaotic environment surrounding the

1989 *Exxon Valdez* oil spill, the largest in U.S. waters until the BP oil disaster of 2010.[38] In exchange for extraction of their resources, Alaska residents enjoy an annual payout of oil royalties from the Alaska Permanent Fund. The state's population has grown steadily since the 1950s and currently stands at about 680,000, with 13 percent Alaska Native.[39] The state has also become strongly Republican, attracting many residents seeking a "frontier" kind of life with allegedly limited government intrusion, an attitude encapsulated by the political views of 2008 vice-presidential candidate and half-term Alaska governor Sarah Palin.

After ANCSA, the U.S. government and state of Alaska considered the native claims issue largely "settled." This was not the feeling of many Alaska Natives, however, who had not been brought into the negotiations at the level of the AFN. From their perspective the ANCSA had, in one swoop, effectively dissolved their aboriginal land claims, made their rights the purview of U.S. law, and superimposed a corporate structure over their subsistence lifestyle. Today the native populations continue to struggle with issues of poverty, sovereignty, and subsistence rights.

As is the case with indigenous communities around the United States, Alaska Native villages are among the poorest in the state. ANCSA projects have brought in some money, but not enough to lift many of the villages above poverty levels.[40] Individuals hold shares in the corporations, enjoy dividends, and vote for tribal corporation directors, but directors are then free to determine the activities of the regional corporations.[41] This has created tensions between regional corporate directors who want to extract natural resources for profit and Alaska Natives who regard such practices as antithetical to traditional subsistence ways. While some regional corporations have been successful through such endeavors as logging, mining, and collaborating with oil companies, others have struggled, finding the abrupt transition from subsistence living to capital accumulation difficult, especially in regions not rich in resources.[42] The disparity in resources is somewhat compensated by a mandated 70 percent sharing of resource revenues among all tribal corporations statewide, but there are still clear discrepancies in regional corporate performance.[43]

Making money is not necessarily the goal of many Alaska Natives, however, particularly those in rural villages more concerned with sovereignty and subsistence rights. While the U.S. government currently recognizes more than two hundred Alaska Native tribal councils, their sovereignty is limited: federal and state Supreme Court decisions in the late 1990s ruled that Alaska Native villages are "sovereigns without territorial reach," with "inherent sovereignty" to regulate domestic affairs but not to extend such rule beyond their territory or people.[44] Left in legally ambiguous gray areas still under contest, village tribal councils frequently have strained relations with regional corporations, due to disputes over resource exploitation and leadership, as well as with the State of Alaska, which is often unresponsive to native rights.[45] There is a "trust relationship" between the federal government and Native American tribes, referring to the federal government's promise— laid out in treaties—to protect and promote tribal self-governance in compensation for the loss of their lands. Native Americans have argued that the trust relationship constitutes legally binding obligations, but the relationship has been interpreted differently and unevenly by U.S. judges.[46]

The struggle for Native American rights is regarded as an early stream of the environmental justice movement. Following the civil rights movement, many inner-city residents, activists, and scholars began calling attention to the concentration within poor and working-class communities of "locally unwanted land uses" such as city dumps, chemical plants, and oil refineries, particularly in communities of color due to the history of residential segregation and discrimination, restricted access to mortgages and loans ("redlining"), zoning practices, and lack of representation on local planning boards.[47] Several studies have shown both race and income to be strong predictors of the location of unwanted land uses.[48]

Awareness of and actions against land-use inequities grew alongside similar struggles, such as the campaign by farmworkers (largely immigrants) to protect themselves against harmful pesticides, the antitoxics movement set off by the contamination of Love Canal, and long-standing indigenous struggles against the overdevelopment of native lands.[49] By the 1990s, these and other struggles had been identified as a broader environmental justice movement (EJM). In contrast to the mainstream environmental movement, the EJM defines "the environment" not as nature per se, but as where people work, live, and play. The EJM is embodied in the numerous, ongoing daily struggles to mitigate harms to human health.[50]

Within the United States, activist and litigation organizations have developed around environmental justice issues, many of them small and grassroots groups that respond to local issues as they develop. The organizations employ a variety of techniques, with litigation just one of several tools including political participation in local development decisions, direct actions, and mobilization of affected communities. The movement's main goal, as articulated by EJM legal advocate Luke Cole, is to "rightly challenge, first and foremost, the legitimacy of the decision-making process and the social structures that allow such decisions to be made without the involvement of those most intimately concerned."[51]

Cole was one of the key lawyers in the Kivalina lawsuit, before a car crash took his life in June 2009. After graduating with a law degree from Harvard, he went on to intern for public rights activist Ralph Nader, and then to cofound the San Francisco–based Center for Race, Poverty, and the Environment in 1989. At the center, Cole worked with communities around the Bay Area and Central Valley of California for cleaner air and water. In 2001, Cole traveled to Kotzebue, Alaska, to help lead a seminar on indigenous environmental law.

At the conference he met residents of Kivalina. They told him about the poisoning of their water by the Red Dog Mine, the world's largest zinc operation, fifty miles east of Kivalina. The mine was a project of Kivalina's regional corporation, NANA, and had become a source of income for NANA, but a source of harm for Kivalina, according to residents. They told Cole that since the mine began operations in 1989, the Wulik River—their primary source of freshwater—sometimes ran in bright colors, tasted funny, and contained many dead and deformed fish. They had reported these problems to NANA and state officials, but nothing had been done. Cole worked with the residents to investigate the mine, found it was in violation of its discharge permits, and filed a lawsuit, leading to a settlement six years later.[52] The long-term health effects from the river's contamination remain to be seen.

According to Luke Cole: "During this time I was going up to Kivalina three, four times a year in the context of this litigation and I was seeing what residents were reporting to me as changes from global warming. I would go up there in September and there was no sea ice. Now, Kivalina is north of the Arctic Circle, and there should be ice but there wasn't. So I asked about it and they said they had been noticing it for many years, but that it had been getting worse."[53]

Despite the long-standing stance of hesitation and skepticism by the executive branch, the U.S. government itself was documenting the effects of climate change in Alaska, particularly on native villages. In

2000, the U.S. Global Change Research Program released its National Assessment Synthesis (NAS) report on climate change, a summary of climate science, which the fossil fuel–based Competitive Enterprise Institute later sued the government for releasing. The report noted Alaska's climate had warmed an average of 4°F since the 1950s, and as much as 7°F in the interior during winter. Permafrost, the permanently frozen subsoil that underlies most of Alaska, was thawing, causing damage to overlying infrastructure and contributing to soil erosion and landslides. Sea ice had retreated 14 percent since 1978 and thinned 40 percent since the 1960s, leaving coastlines vulnerable to erosion and flooding.[54]

The NAS report also noted that climate change was already affecting life in Alaska Native villages.[55] In December 2003, the Government Accountability Office (GAO) went on to report that most of Alaska's more than two hundred native villages were affected to some degree by flooding and erosion, with thirty-one facing imminent threats "due in part to rising temperatures that cause protective shore ice to form later in the year, leaving the villages vulnerable to storms."[56]

As with the pollution from Red Dog Mine, the people of Kivalina had reported the effects of warming temperatures, but had not received any concrete assistance to mitigate risks to their safety from erosion. They had voted to relocate in 1992, petitioned various government bodies to begin a relocation process, and hit a dead end. Meanwhile the need to relocate grew more urgent as the effects of climate change accelerated the village's erosion and left residents increasingly in danger from storms.

Similar effects were impacting indigenous communities throughout the Arctic. In 2005, an Inuit petition was filed with the Inter-American Commission on Human Rights, created in 1959 to uphold and investigate violations of the 1948 American Declaration of the Rights and Duties of Man. The Inuit petition alleged the U.S. government was violating the human rights of Arctic people by refusing to limit greenhouse gas emissions. Seeking caps on U.S. emissions, the petition also called for the commission to produce plans to protect Inuit culture and resources through adaptation assistance. The petition was rejected one year later by the commission, which maintained that the charges outlined in the petition were insufficiently supported for making a determination.[57] The same year, the U.S. Army Corps of Engineers issued a report stating the situation in Kivalina was "dire" and that the entire town needed to be immediately relocated,[58] at an estimated cost ranging from $100 million to $400 million, according to various government estimates.[59]

To counter the government stalling and corporate indifference, residents of the village began debating other options for protecting themselves. Cole suggested a climate change lawsuit, positioning the situation within an environmental justice framework, as the only way to give the people of Kivalina a voice, however imperfect the suit might be. "No one asked the people of Kivalina, y'know, 'Would you like to have your environment ruined?' A lawsuit is the only way they have of expressing themselves in the environmental justice process," Cole explained in a July 2008 interview. "It's late in the day, it's inadequate, it's a blunt tool, it's the only tool they have left."[60]

Cole spoke to lawyer Heather Kendall-Miller of the Native American Rights Fund (NARF), which provides legal representation for Native Americans. Working in Anchorage, Kendall-Miller was acutely aware of the climate change issues facing native villages and interested in branching out legally in that area, but had not yet found a way. "My primary line of work is litigating subsistence and tribal sovereignty

cases. Climate change is outside [NARF's] scope, but it became necessary when we saw how drastic the effects were on the people that we
work with and serve," she said in late August 2008.[61] She noted that
while the federal government has a trust relationship with Kivalina, it
would be difficult to legally enforce federal assistance with the village's
relocation, making her receptive to pursuing the case as a matter of environmental pollution and public nuisance.[62]

Kendall-Miller had already been approached about such a possibility by Matt Pawa, a lawyer at a small Boston firm that had filed the first
federal global warming nuisance case with attorneys general in *Connecticut v. AEP.* Together Cole, Kendall-Miller, and Pawa considered
filing a claim on behalf of Kivalina and discussed this option with the
village. After several meetings, the Kivalina City and Tribal Councils
agreed. Pawa then recruited Steve Berman and Steve Susman, both
high-profile litigators involved in the state tobacco lawsuits—Berman
on the side of states and Susman on the side of tobacco companies—as
well as several other public rights lawyers.

On February 26, 2008, Kivalina, in both capacities as a native village
and city, filed a legal claim in the United States District Court for the
Northern District of California against twenty-four oil, electricity, and
coal companies: ExxonMobil, BP, BP America, BP Products, Chevron
Corporation, Chevron USA, ConocoPhillips, Royal Dutch Shell, Shell
Oil, Peabody Energy, AES Corporation, American Electric Power
Company, American Electric Power Services Corporation, DTE En-
ergy Company, Duke Energy, Dynegy Holdings, Edison International,
MidAmerican Energy Holdings Company, Mirant Corporation, NRG
Energy, Pinnacle West Capital Corporation, Reliant Energy, Southern
Company, and Xcel Energy. The claim alleges that the defendants are
significant contributors of greenhouse gas emissions, exacerbating global

warming and the erosion in Kivalina, constituting a public nuisance under federal and state common law. The suit seeks damages of up to $400 million, the estimated cost of relocating the village. In addition, there are secondary claims of conspiracy and concert of action against ExxonMobil, AEP, BP, Chevron, ConocoPhillips, Duke, Peabody, and Southern Company for conspiring to create a false scientific debate about climate change to deceive the public. The defendants in the first claim were selected for being among the largest emitters of greenhouse gases, while those in the secondary claim were selected for, in the words of Luke Cole, "going above and beyond" in their efforts to deceive the public about global warming.[63]

The lawsuit cuts across many aspects of climate change, as illustrated by the different but interconnected motivations of the lawyers who filed the claim. Steve Susman, for example, is particularly focused on addressing climate change, and holding fossil fuel companies accountable, similar to the tobacco lawsuits. His involvement in the Kivalina case is notable both because he is a high-profile litigator who charges up to a thousand dollars an hour for his services, and because he was involved in the tobacco suits—on the side of tobacco. In interviews, Susman has attributed his interest in global warming to his wife who, during a May 2009 interview, was correcting him or adding tidbits in the background as he and I spoke. He briefly recapped his growing interest in climate change: "In the fall of 2005, I was with my wife and helping her organize a Yale conference on climate change. I went with her and didn't know anything about it and started reading materials on the plane and it sounded very interesting to me, it sounded a lot like tobacco had sounded, and so I just right then and there, and a bit at my wife's urging, decided it was something I was going to get interested in."[64] Shortly afterward, Susman worked pro bono to help thirty-seven Texas cities stop the construction of coal-burning electric utility plants in the state.

Susman saw many parallels with the tobacco suits in the form of the misinformation campaigns, but also recognized that such tactics can be hard to prosecute:

> It's very much a legal gray area. Companies enjoy a First Amendment right to petition the government and speak their minds, it's part of free speech. Even if they are saying it in conspiracy and collusion with one another, as long as they are saying things, expressing opinions, it is protected by the First Amendment. And that's clearly an argument [defendant companies] are making against us in this case, that we are just complaining about something that is protected by the First Amendment, the Noerr-Pennington doctrine, so I think it is very difficult under existing law to hold companies responsible for promulgating bad science. Laws can be passed but right now it is very difficult to hold people responsible for promulgating junk science. However, to the extent that there is a good faith belief on their part, they enjoy that right, so we could try to prove they knew the information they were spreading was false and being used to deliberately influence public opinion—that would override their First Amendment rights.[65]

This is why, Susman said, lawyers prosecuting such cases strive to reach the discovery phase of a lawsuit in order to demonstrate industry knowledge of the falsity of their claims. Indeed, public health historians Barry Castleman, David Rosner, Gerald Markowitz, and David Michaels all affirm such documents have been crucial to their research. Without documentation, allegations that corporations know they are misrepresenting science remain in the realm of speculation, in both the court of law and, in many ways, the court of public opinion. Steve Berman, who helped gain the release of the internal documents of tobacco manufacturer Liggett and secure the industry's settlement of the state suits leading up to the master national settlement,[66] believes concrete evidence of industry knowledge is an important factor but not in itself sufficient to bring about successful liability: "The first forty years of tobacco, they won every case, despite evidence of harm."[67] The first step to a successful claim, he said, was having a case reach the discovery and trial stage, which was being prevented by judges invoking the political question doctrine: "What is or isn't a nuisance is something that courts have struggled with for over a hundred years. If you want to point to a particular law in effect, that is a preemption issue, but I don't think a proper analysis is the political question. With a political question, everything gets knocked out, you don't have to deal with the other issues."[68]

Defendant companies, in their response, split up into three groups: power, oil, and coal. Each group filed multiple motions to dismiss, employing similar arguments, most of them common to the prior global warming lawsuits: the claims were barred by preemption, the political question doctrine, and lack of legal standing. Although none of the defendant lawyers agreed to an interview or to be quoted, some spoke to me to help clarify the specifics of the legal arguments in the motions. If the judge were to accept the defendant motions for dismissal, Kivalina's lawsuit would be thrown out before going to the discovery and trial phase.

Although hired by the defendant companies, defendant law firms are in many ways business associates of the corporations they defend, beyond providing legal defense. Several of the law firms, such as Baker Botts (representing Dynegy and Reliant Energy), Jones Day (Xcel Energy), King & Spalding (Chevron), Sidley & Austin (Duke and American Electric), and Hunton & Williams (DTE, Edison, MidAmerican Energy, Pinnacle West, and Southern Company), were established in the early to mid-1800s and developed alongside the fossil fuel industry, expanding their own power and influence by helping these industries grow.

Their partners sit on the boards of defendant companies and serve in government positions related to management and oversight of the fossil fuel and defense industries. Former King & Spalding senior partner and former Georgia Democratic senator Sam Nunn is currently on the board of directors of Chevron, the company King & Spalding is representing in *Kivalina*. Former Sidley & Austin partner and utility lobbyist James Connaughton served as the chair of George W. Bush's Council on Environmental Quality, fighting against the Kyoto accords, and, upon leaving that position, went to work for an energy company. Former senior partner James Baker of Baker Botts was appointed Bush's Special Presidential Envoy to Iraq, in which capacity he transferred Iraq's unpaid debt to a consortium involving his company, the Carlyle Group,[69] also co-owned by the Bush family.[70] In short, many partners of defendant law firms have been tied to the same political-economic interests that benefit their clients. When they argue that U.S. policy on climate change has been adequate and sufficient, they are discussing a policy that some of their former partners and business associates have helped shape.

Other defendant law firms are part of the PDI or have actively shaped the product defense strategies of the tobacco and/or fossil fuel industries. BP's representation Arnold & Porter, as mentioned, founded the public relations firm APCO Worldwide, which helped pioneer efforts against "junk science" and civil lawsuits.[71] Former Sidley & Austin partner Christopher DeMuth was the longtime president (1986–2008) of the ExxonMobil-funded think tank the American Enterprise Institute, which offered money to scientists and economists for articles undermining IPCC reports.[72] King & Spalding partner Katherine Rhyne served on the executive council of the Harvard Center for Risk Analysis, a regular producer of cost-benefit analyses that portray industry regulations as unnecessary and economically disastrous.[73]

Oral arguments over the motions to dismiss were scheduled for May 2009, but Judge Saundra Armstrong of the Northern District of California announced that a hearing would not be necessary. As both sides waited for her to issue a ruling, a sudden shift came in climate change legislation: on September 21, 2009, the trial court decision in *Connecticut v. AEP* was overturned. Judges Peter Hall and Joseph McLaughlin of the Second Circuit Court of Appeals (the third justice, Sonia Sotomayor, was not part of the decision, as she was appointed to the Supreme Court) argued that the federal public nuisance claim was not barred by the political question doctrine, and that the plaintiffs had legal standing to sue.[74] In their judgment, the claim in *AEP* was not constrained by the *Baker* political question test because "nowhere in their complaint do Plaintiffs ask the court to fashion a comprehensive and far-reaching solution to global climate change."[75] Rather than regarding U.S. action on global warming as constituting a clear policy, as previous courts had, this court instead wondered, "What exactly *is* U.S. 'policy' on greenhouse gas emissions?"[76] and noted that while U.S. policy is far from unified, it is certainly not in favor of *increasing* emissions, making adjudication not inconsistent with the direction of the political branches. The Second Circuit found that states and citizens with discrete, identifiable harms have legal standing to bring federal public nuisance suits over climate change, opening the door for future global warming suits.

The finding seemed to bode well for Kivalina residents. Judge Saundra Armstrong, however, was not persuaded. Nine days later, on September 30, 2009, Judge Armstrong issued a ruling in which she noted the finding of the Second Circuit, but then stated, "This Court is not so sanguine."[77] Instead, Judge Armstrong decided that the political question doctrine did apply, arguing that the *Kivalina* claim necessarily involves cost-benefit analyses that the executive and legislative branches must speak to before the judicial branch can act, satisfying the six-point *Baker* test and preventing adjudication.

Judge Armstrong also went on to deny the village of Kivalina its legal standing to bring the case, arguing that global warming is too ubiquitous to be "fairly traceable" to the defendants' emissions, as required for legal standing, and that while states have the right to bring public nuisance suits, Kivalina does not, thereby denying Kivalina's rights as a sovereign nation. In dismissing Kivalina's claim on grounds of both political question and legal standing, Judge Armstrong declined to address the secondary claims of civil conspiracy and concert of action. The actions of defendant fossil fuel companies in denying climate change went unaddressed.

The *Kivalina* decision was a rebuke of the Second Circuit Court of Appeals in *AEP*. The rationale of the *AEP* Appeals Court was reinforced only a few weeks later, however, when the district court decision in *Comer v. Murphy Oil Co.* was also reversed.[78] The claim, a class action against petrochemical companies filed by victims of Hurricane Katrina, had been dismissed on political question and legal standing grounds. On October 16, 2009, Judges Eugene Davis, Carl Stewart, and James Dennis of the Fifth Circuit Court of Appeals ruled that the plaintiffs did have legal standing to bring public and private nuisance, trespass, and negligence claims (private nuisance being interference with the rights of specific people, trespass a direct or causal intrusion into another person's property, and negligence a failure to protect from foreseeable risks of harm). The judges, however, denied the secondary claims addressing the misinformation campaign by fossil fuel companies because the alleged harms from the campaign are "a generalized grievance that is more properly dealt with by the representative branches and common to all consumers of petrochemicals and the American public," rather than a particularized harm suited for the courts.[79]

Regarding the political question doctrine, the *Comer* judges found that the district courts, including Judge Armstrong although she was not named, had incorrectly interpreted the Supreme Court's decision in the 1984 case *Chevron v. Natural Resources Defense Council.* The district judges had taken the Supreme Court ruling to mean federal courts in air pollution cases must necessarily balance social and economic interests in the manner of a legislative body.[80] The *Comer* judges, however, stated that the Supreme Court was referring to legislative—not judicial—duties, as such an approach would render courts unable to rule on any air pollution cases.[81] The reversal of *Comer* is particularly notable because it is a private class action for compensatory and punitive damages that resulted from a hurricane, typically considered a "natural" disaster,[82] which would open the door to private-party lawsuits from the growing number of people affected by climate change.

Shortly after these rulings, Steve Susman told me Kivalina would be appealing the trial court decision. He saw the reversals of *AEP* and *Comer* as good signs for the people of Kivalina, and found it unfortunate that Kivalina's claim had been dismissed despite the *AEP* reversal and the later *Comer* decision, pending at the time. Kivalina legal counsel Brent Newell of the Center for Race, Poverty, and the Environment said the obstacles and slow pace involved with common law, as evidenced by Kivalina's claim, point to the need for a more democratic law, one easier to access by those harmed. Yet impending legislation on climate change looks to be even more complex than common law. Said Newell, "Cap and trade will result in an extremely complicated system, analogous to the Clean Air Act's New Source Review [NSR] permitting program for areas that don't meet health-based air quality standards. NSR has become an area dominated by dense legal requirements and technical hurdles. Cap and trade will become a realm dominated by attorneys and consultants, leaving the public out of the loop and disempowered, for they cannot possibly afford to participate at that level."[83]

The reversal of *AEP* opened the door for the possibility of a public nuisance lawsuit against fossil fuel companies, offering a means of holding them accountable as the inevitable public harms from climate change grow. It is notable, however, that the *AEP* claim did not raise conspiracy charges, and those in *Comer* and *Kivalina* were thrown out. As the examples of asbestos, lead, and tobacco suggest, proof and consideration of corporate malfeasance, although not sufficient for a guilty verdict, are often necessary for one. Yet when it comes to climate change, legal consideration of the corporate role in advancing false science to sway public opinion appears far off.

On February 26, 2010, the Fifth Circuit court for *Comer* decided to review the appeal with the full court. Only one month later, however, a five-member majority of the Fifth Circuit issued an order dismissing the review of the appeal, since the circuit court lacked a quorum, reportedly because several judges owned stock in the defendant companies and recused themselves. The original dismissal of *Comer* now stands. Then, on December 6, 2010, the Supreme Court announced it would be conducting a judicial review of the *AEP* case, raising questions as to how the court will rule on issues of legal standing, preemption, and political question, which could have large ramifications for all climate change lawsuits, including *Kivalina*.

With Kivalina's claim dismissed for now and the fate of future climate change lawsuits uncertain, the village's longtime residents must look to other means to protect themselves and their homeland.

OVER THE YEARS, NUMEROUS studies were conducted to investigate new village site options for the people of Kivalina. The City of Kivalina, the Northwest Arctic Borough, and the Native Village of Kivalina began a partnership with the U.S. Army Corps of Engineers (USACE)–Alaska District to work toward moving the entire community off the barrier island to a new village site. The people of Kivalina voted for Kiniktuuraq, a site just two miles away.

The studies officially began in 1990 and continued for years. During the study process, many contentious issues were raised. Outside influences hampered the efforts of the local leadership—the Kivalina City Council and the Kivalina Indian Reorganization Act (IRA) Councils—to move forward. The site selected by the community members of the village was cost-prohibitive, according to the USACE, due to the permafrost conditions. Those conditions, they said, would require a gravel pad of up to nine feet high. The USACE contended that the U.S. government would never fund such a move that would benefit only a small handful of Inupiaq people.

—KIVALINA TRIBAL ADMINISTRATOR COLLEEN SWAN

SIX

RELOCATION IN A NEOLIBERAL STATE

As the first big fall storm approached in 2004, the ground behind [the school principal's] trailer collapsed. Where there had once been a broad beach between the town and the ocean, the earth behind the buildings now dropped directly into the water, and former school principal Gerry Pickner suddenly found his home teetering on a steep bank with seawater splashing against its windows. While teachers scrambled to move his belongings into the school, the ocean advanced on the town's fuel tanks and generators; meanwhile, at the island's north end, waves threatened a gravel airstrip, Kivalina's main connection to the outside world.[1]

—David Darlington, *Reader's Digest*

Being hit by storm after storm, each quickly eroding more of the village, has had a marked effect on Kivalina's people. Enoch Adams, chairman of the Kivalina Relocation Committee, said flatly, "Our people here have lost their peace of mind because of what has been taking place here with the storms."[2] Historically, sea ice provided protection from fall storms, but for the past three decades in Kivalina the ice has been forming later in the year and melting earlier, leaving the shoreline exposed and vulnerable. Heavy rainfalls in recent years have swallowed as much as seventy feet of land in the course of one storm.[3] Despite several U.S. government reports stating that Kivalina and other Alaska Native communities must be relocated due to the effects of climate change, there is no specific policy in place for relocation and no agency tasked with overseeing the effort, even as the situation facing many of these communities has reached an emergency management stage. Yet emergency management resources are currently not sufficient to secure the village's safe relocation, and some political representatives are looking to further cut the scope of all disaster management efforts.

Until recently, disasters were often thought of as either natural or technological in nature, and necessarily disruptive of a preexisting social order.[4] It has been increasingly observed, however, that a particular social "order" itself can lead to disaster. For example, social actions such as extracting coal and oil, clear-cutting forests, and developing on wetlands and coastlines that might otherwise buffer storms all create risks that could become disaster.[5] Given this intermeshing of the social world and the natural environment, many disasters can more accurately be described as socio-natural events, with the degree of individual and community vulnerability affected by political-economic factors, such as access to stable housing, insurance, reliable health care, and responsive political representation.[6]

The federal government's role in disasters began with aiding communities during major crises, an early example being the army's assistance during a large New Hampshire fire in 1802.[7] As the United States had few government agencies in the early 1800s, the army continued to assist local communities after large disasters. For additional assistance, the federal government developed a patchwork of programs and funds for community aid and redevelopment,[8] ultimately leading to the creation of the Federal Emergency Management Agency (FEMA) in 1979. Since its inception FEMA has played a dual role, providing domestic assistance for both "natural" and human threats to the nation. In 1980, President Ronald Reagan focused the agency's efforts on defense and Cold War exercises over socio-natural disasters, with the former dominating FEMA spending twelve to one by 1985. George H. W. Bush maintained this focus, leaving FEMA unprepared to respond to Hurricane Hugo in 1989 and Hurricane Andrew in 1992. (Not long after, Bush lost the Florida vote and the 1992 presidential election.[9]) After Bush, President Clinton and FEMA director James Lee Witt redirected FEMA's focus back to socio-natural disasters, and the agency quickly transformed from what South Carolina senator Ernest Hollings had described as a "bunch of bureaucratic jackasses" into a dependable institution that enjoyed widespread bipartisan support.[10] FEMA's role took a sharp turn after the attacks of September 11, 2001, however, as it was quickly placed under the control of the newly created Department of Homeland Security (DHS).[11]

The stated goal of the DHS is to prepare for, prevent, and respond to domestic emergencies, particularly terrorism. Most DHS funds are therefore delegated to operations against perceived terrorist threats. The remaining "natural" disaster funds have been increasingly awarded to military and intelligence contractors seeking larger roles in all types of disaster management.[12] The idea that military contractors would be appropriate facilitators of disaster management is aided by the "disaster mythology,"[13] the belief that during disasters people panic and social order breaks down, requiring top-down, external control.[14] This myth remains pervasive despite consistent research showing that people actually demonstrate high levels of cooperative, active, and adaptive behavior during disasters.[15] The misconception has allowed the defense and intelligence sectors to position themselves as crucial disaster management experts, directing funds away from community efforts and resulting in what some have called "the disaster after the disaster."[16]

Hurricane Katrina was a clear example of the new face of top-down disaster management. The private military contractor Blackwater (now Xe) was paid at least $73 million for its government-contracted work in the wake of Katrina[17]; its primary duties were to protect government projects and private properties, apparently from New Orleans residents themselves.[18] Such policing, in line with the disaster mythology, was implemented despite widespread reports of cooperative and resourceful behavior among residents.[19] Meanwhile, many post-Katrina disaster funds, originally generated to help communities rebuild themselves, were siphoned toward gentrification projects and the enrichment of already wealthy institutions, or in some cases were never distributed at all.[20]

The majority of disaster assistance and funding is also only made available after disaster strikes, with much less funding allocated for risk mitigation and community preparedness.[21] Kivalina was eligible for little aid until their situation became dangerous.

As the first of the 2004 fall storms hit Kivalina, the wind produced waves that topped the sea bank, flowing into the village and filling the streets with water. Former Kivalina school principal Gerry Pickner suddenly found the land in front of his home had dropped away. Ralph Knox, a Kivalina resident and artist who lives on the western coast of the island, told me that during the storm "the water got up to my door. Right here." He pointed to his doorstep. "And it raised the [floor] boards of that house," he said, pointing to a small, wooden home next to his.[22] Water crept onto Kivalina's airstrip, threatening to strand the village. In desperation, residents sawed apart a plane that had crash-landed several years earlier, using the sheet metal to shield the runway.

After the storm, the community helped relocate the principal's home parallel to the school, a bit further from the sea. But calm was short-lived. In October 2005, another storm hit. The rain, wind, and waves pounded the coastline, causing significant erosion up to the school and the principal's housing unit. Residents and school staff acted quickly to place anything they could between the sea and the school building, to act as a makeshift barrier. The situation was described in detail on the City of Kivalina's website:

Kivalina homes by the shoreline, 2008

Empty 55 gallon barrels are gathered by the scene and school maintenance personnel have the tools to open the tops so they can be filled with gravel. Women and children alike volunteer to fill sandbags with gravel from the school's old drainfield. The men are down below the bank placing the sandbags inside the barrels with waves crashing around them.... The wind storm continues and the airport is now in danger and is rapidly eroding from the fierce waves. This time, it must be the work of men as the space is limited. They try anything, including remnants of a plane. Those are taken out to sea as if they were foam material. Finally, in a desperate attempt to control the erosion, someone remembers the 8 x 24 metal sheets sitting outside of the watertank farm. There are four sheets and all are placed individually in a line on the banks near the airport. They work through the night in the dark to place them into position. Finally, towards morning, they are all in place and the erosion stops with only twelve feet to spare from the airport.[23]

The village was declared a disaster area, and FEMA provided funding for sandbags to help prevent further erosion. Clearly, more than sandbags were needed, and Kivalina's precarious situation was shared by many other Alaska Native villages. In response, Congress passed Section 117 in the 2005 Consolidated Appropriations Act, which allowed the Army Corps of Engineers to carry out storm damage protection projects for Alaska Native villages at full federal expense, waiving the usual cost-sharing requirement. In 2006 Tom Bolen, public services director of the village's local representation, the Northwest Arctic Borough, helped the native corporation subsidiary NANA Pacific secure a contract to construct a protective seawall for Kivalina. The actions of NANA Pacific, however, ultimately placed the community in even more danger.

While many regional tribal corporations struggled, NANA Regional Corporation became profitable through resource extraction. In 1978, NANA formed a partnership with a major mining company to develop a large zinc and lead mine in northwest Alaska, on lands allotted to NANA through the ANCSA. The mine became Red Dog,

Sandbags to armor the coast, 2008

whose discharges proceeded to pollute Kivalina's water. In 1989, NANA joined several other Alaska Native corporations in a partnership with BP for oil extraction in the North Slope, the uppermost area of Alaska (northeast of Kivalina), with the petroleum transported via the Trans-Alaska Pipeline system to Valdez, the site of the Exxon oil spill that same year. In addition to resource extraction, NANA also ventured into government contract services. To help struggling native corporations, the late Alaska senator Ted Stevens created exemptions in the 1980s making it easier for tribal corporations to secure large, no-bid federal contracts.

After the attacks of September 11, 2001, NANA established a subsidiary, NANA Pacific LLC, to seek contracts with the newly created DHS. According to its website, NANA Pacific provides services for the DHS and projects in emergency preparedness and response, as well as management and consulting for Department of Defense agencies such as the U.S. Northern Command (created in 2002, after the attacks of September 11, 2001) and the National Guard.

A 2004 *Mother Jones* investigation found that private contractors such as Halliburton were creating joint ventures with tribal corporations to receive more, and more favorable, government contracts, as tribal corporations have unlimited rights to "sole-source" federal contracts (those not put up for competitive bid).[24] While this measure was ostensibly implemented to benefit Alaska Natives, the joint-venture status lets regional corporations staff non-native company employees as their own, meaning few Alaska Natives may actually be involved in the contract work, as either workers or executive officers.[25] Senator Stevens, in fact, lobbied to remove the requirement that the tribal corporation receiving the contract have an Alaska Native as chief executive officer.[26] (Recently, there have been calls to abolish the program altogether rather than ensure it does what it was supposed to do—namely, benefit Alaska Natives.)

For Kivalina, NANA Pacific hired Drake Construction to build the seawall. The plan was to use HESCO Concertainers, also known as gabion baskets, an erosion-control product that Bolen, the Northwest Arctic Borough public services director, assured Kivalina residents had been used successfully in other parts of the state.[27] To fill the HESCO baskets, members of the Drake crew were instructed to extract sand and gravel from the beach directly in front of the village's fuel tanks and airport, despite warnings by residents that doing so would cause erosion to the bank. Kivalina residents hired to help construct the wall also argued that the material for the wall would be ineffective, as it amounted to nothing more than mesh baskets. Their warnings were ignored. According to Kivalina resident Reppi Swan of Kivalina Erosion Control: "When we were building the wall there were a bunch of guys that tried to tell [NANA Pacific] that putting the sand in the baskets wouldn't work. A whole bunch of us told them it wouldn't work, but they didn't listen to us. The contractors that built it—Drake—the guys that were contracted knew it wouldn't work either but they were being paid."[28]

A ceremony was set for October 12, 2006, to celebrate the wall's completion, but the day before, a windstorm and powerful undertow from the sea pulled the sand out from underneath the baskets. The event was canceled. Within a month, the sea had completely dismantled the multimillion-dollar barrier. Tribal administrator Colleen Swan had foreseen such a result: "We had absolutely no voice for the project that came in 2006: wire baskets, filled with sand, and no bottom. One on top of the other, no bottom, and the waves just sucked out the sand from the bottom."[29]

Two days after the planned celebration, Senator Stevens went with Tom Bolen and other government officials to assess the damage done to the wall, all of them appearing incredulous, much to the exasperation of the local residents whose warnings had been dismissed. The Army Corps later concluded that the wall had not only failed, but in fact accelerated Kivalina's erosion.[30] With the barrier destroyed, the village was left largely unprotected until a new erosion protection project by the Army Corps began construction in 2008.[31]

In September 2007, Kivalina officials received a fax from the National Weather Service reporting winds in the area were expected to hit with a wave height of up to eight feet. Without a seawall, the village faced the danger of a spill from their fourteen large fuel tanks. There was also nowhere for residents to go if the village flooded, so the

Northwest Arctic Borough decided to initiate a precautionary evacua
tion. Those wishing to leave were transported via cargo planes and off-
road vehicles. Some residents remained, either by choice or to help
protect the seawall and village.

Kivalina residents Dolly and Reppi Swan, and their friend David
Frankson, vividly recalled the 2007 storm. Sitting at a table in the Swans'
home while their children ran around us playing, Dolly said, "It was
kinda scary, it's hard to put into words. It was so different to watch that
big storm coming in. You would not want to be around here. It's like, I
wanted to get on the first plane out of here. But I stayed. Reppi asked me
to, he wanted me to be with him. We sent our children to be evacuated."[32]

Reppi, in turn, stayed because his father instructed him to, as part
of his duties with Kivalina Erosion Control. He worked during the
storm protecting the shoreline: "The work was dangerous. One time
before the storm we were setting bags into the water and one of the guys
was setting bags and tripped right into the water. He was getting so
used to it, running down, taking bags and bringing them back up, and
the bags have loops on them, when he started running down his feet got
caught, and he fell right into the water. So we grabbed him."[33]

David Frankson helped the people of Kivalina evacuate. While
trying to move the people out, he encountered difficulties: "We were
supposed to go to Kotzebue but the FAA [Federal Aviation Adminis-
tration] said no…. They said the pilots could not exceed their hours.
So we took our four-wheelers down to Red Dog Mine. Men, women,
and children. But the children were too young to go there, it was very
dangerous."[34] Other residents took on more of the emotional labor
during the evacuation, such as resident Margaret Baldwin: "It was really scary, some children were crying, without their parents, I had to
comfort them, comfort the children. Small kids."[35]

After the storm, the Army Corps approved construction of a large rock revetment project for Kivalina, contracted to Brice Construction of Fairbanks, a local company that specializes in remote Alaska areas. The wall was being constructed when I first visited Kivalina. Army Corps representative Eric Schneider, acting as supervisor of the wall's construction, was optimistic about the project and its engineering design. Drawing a diagram in the sand as we stood atop the construction site, he explained that the revetment was constructed at an angle, so that if waves disrupted the revetment, rocks would spill into the disturbed area and re-secure it.[36] He was realistic, however, about the wall's potential: "Oh, it will buy the people here ten, fifteen years. It's not a permanent solution."

According to Patricia Opheen, chief of the engineering division for the Army Corps of Engineers in the Alaska District, "We have emphasized that that structure would sustain much longer than fifteen years with minimal maintenance, it's just without any maintenance it's inevitable that there will be storms that relocate some of the rock and not have the armor rock covering the smaller material underneath it."

Rock revetment, 2008

She did not, however, see long-term, continued maintenance as necessarily desirable or reliable, given the uncertainty of continued congressional funding. She also stressed that the revetment could not provide full protection: "The rock revetment will only protect against erosion, it will not do anything for flooding, so a storm surge coming in could still flood the community."[37]

The rock revetment was initially designed to be 3,200 feet long and completed over a period of approximately ten years.[38] Funding, however, was only secured for 1,600 feet on the sea side of the village, where the fuel tanks had been relocated. Then, in 2009, Section 117 was rescinded, putting further construction of the rock revetment in question, as the Army Corps no longer had authorized funding for its completion. It is not known why the funding was repealed.[39]

Left unaddressed was the lagoon side of the island, so severely undercut that one turquoise-blue home hangs precariously off the edge, reinforced with sandbags. When I asked one of its residents, Andy Baldwin, if he was nervous about erosion, he said, "Yes, I have nightmares [about] being taken out to sea."[40] Swatting gently at a large group of mosquitoes buzzing around his face, he then asked me what I thought he should do, because the situation was confusing and he wasn't sure. I shrugged helplessly, not knowing what to tell him. The Army Corps later began construction on an additional four hundred feet of the revetment on the lagoon side.

As I spoke to residents, it was clear that they were acutely aware of what was happening to their village and the danger facing them. Margaret Baldwin was particularly vivid in her description: "The village is getting narrower and narrower and it's eroding underneath, like the bottom of a tornado, like a funnel."[41]

Kivalina home held up with sandbags, 2008

Margaret's friend, Emma Adams, sat by her side and nodded. "The village is standing on, underneath, it's like gravel. Like sand or gravel." She looked at me. "That's what we think. You can notice it's getting more narrow every year, from both sides. It's going to get to the point where some day we will have to relocate ourselves. So the seawall, the [revetment] project, I hope it helps."[42]

Village elder Joe Swan expressed a similar sense of waiting for the impending danger: "This erosion started in 1952. That's when it started. Not that much, but it was eroding, slowly. But recently, it's very fast, and if you look at old pictures, the shoreline, the erosion is coming in fast. That's why they have to put up protection, because it was close to the [fuel] tanks. The erosion was so fast we had to move the tanks. Everything is just standing."[43]

Other residents said they were not scared, but were pessimistic about relocation. Artist Russell Adams Jr., who makes carvings from whalebone, said, "I don't get nervous with the storms. I've seen big ones, small ones, all my life, forty-something years. But the erosion is getting worse. This is my home, but I want to move. Real bad. But we don't have the money. Not with the [Iraq] war. And Ted Stevens with this bullshit [corruption charges]. He's the one that finds us money. We'll never move."[44]

The relocation process has been ongoing since 1992, when the village first voted in favor of it. Since then, Kivalina residents have struggled to find government assistance and aid for their relocation, reminiscent of earlier U.S. communities facing disaster, sifting through a patchwork of government programs and agencies to locate and apply for the appropriate assistance.[45] FEMA was created to address precisely this lack of a centralized disaster management agency, but it does not formally manage relocations; according to the GAO, no government agency does.[46] I asked Mike McKinnon of the Denali Commission, a government body that works with rural Alaska communities, about FEMA's involvement in Kivalina's relocation. He said, "FEMA is in the business of responding to emergencies and I haven't seen them part of the proactive 'let's get people moved and where would they be moved to' effort. They respond to emergencies that come up."[47] FEMA's involvement in relocation is not without precedent: After the large Midwestern flood of 1993, FEMA bought out Illinois and Missouri floodplain properties at a cost of $56.3 million and relocated the town of Valmeyer, Illinois. The agency's involvement in the relocation, however, occurred after disaster had struck.[48]

Although the federal government does not have a formal process in place for relocation, Kivalina was able to initiate a master plan to determine the possibilities for relocation. This report would also facilitate federal assistance by documenting whether Kivalina's relocation would meet the requirements for federally sponsored projects under the National Environmental Policy Act.[49] The master plan was undertaken by the Army Corps, but contracted to Tryck Nyman Hayes (TNH), an engineering, construction, and technical services organization based in Alaska.

After receiving the contract, TNH was acquired by URS Corporation, a private engineering and technical services corporation that lobbies heavily and has been granted many government contracts, both in homeland security and overseas military operations. The URS board of directors includes former general Joseph Ralston, the U.S. Special Envoy for countering the Kurdistan Workers Party and a director for defense contractor Lockheed Martin, and former senator Bill Frist, who coauthored a bill denying habeas corpus rights to those suspected of terrorist activities. URS has been charged with negligence, accused of overlooking key vulnerabilities in its safety assessment of the Minnesota I-35W Bridge before it collapsed in 2007, killing thirteen people. The company settled but did not admit fault. In 2004, FEMA contracted out its hurricane disaster plan for Louisiana to three private companies, among them URS. Together, before Katrina hit, the companies did a mock hurricane simulation, "Hurricane Pam," based on a category three storm.[50] Afterward, the FEMA website declared the Pam exercise "great progress," making no mention of the private companies involved. URS was paid $500,000 for the exercise. Only a few months later, an actual category three storm—Hurrricane Katrina—hit and proceeded to decimate New Orleans, suggesting that however successful the Pam simulation had been, the efforts were not matched in the implementation.

Kivalina voted in 1992 to begin a relocation process, and in 1998 to move the village to Igrugaivik, along the Wulik River, which flows into the Kivalina Lagoon. The idea, however, was scrapped after an Army Corps study suggested the Igrugaivik site was too unstable.[51] On April 10, 2000, a special election was held in Kivalina to choose a new relocation site. Kiniktuuraq (across the channel) received 53 votes, Imnaaquq (along the Kivalina River) received 32 votes, remaining in Kivalina received 8 votes, and the aforementioned Igrugaivik got 6 votes.[52] The chosen site, Kiniktuuraq, is a mile southeast of the village and has long been used by residents as a camping ground during hunting trips.

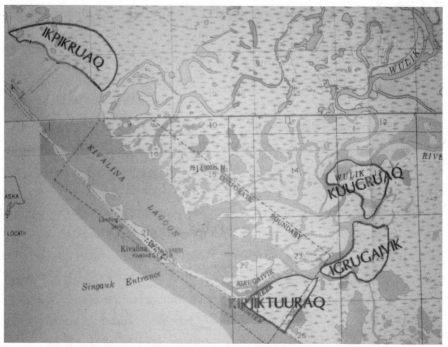

Map of Kivalina and possible relocation sites, 2008

When TNH/URS undertook the master plan for Kivalina's relocation, they evaluated six sites, among them Kiniktuuraq, and concluded that the site was "vulnerable to erosion and must be armored using armor rock and riprap on those sides."[53] This frustrated Kivalina residents, as it conflicted with and disregarded their traditional knowledge of the area.

According to Reppi Swan, "What the elders say is when it flooded here, it didn't flood in Kiniktuuraq. But the Army Corps and some other big companies say that it's [Kiniktuuraq] a floodplain. But to our traditional knowledge it didn't flood when it flooded around here. The majority, 70 percent, of people voted to move there, and the process was going and going until some people said it was going to flood over there, and the Army Corps and all those other companies believed that. And it stopped the process."[54] If Kiniktuuraq were declared vulnerable to erosion, it would require sand nourishment to qualify for any government assistance and insurance, raising the cost of relocation.

Enoch Adams also disagreed with the URS report. "Some of the conclusions in [the master plan] are erroneous at best. There is a conclusion that states that Kiniktuuraq is in a floodplain. We know that is not true. Of course living and growing up around here you get a sense of what's around you, where you live, and when we go to that area that the community picked we know it's higher than the current site, I think it's between five and ten feet higher."[55]

The idea that contractors would know more about the cold and remote Arctic than longtime residents is debatable, raising questions of authority and knowledge.[56] Although traditional knowledge is often viewed as different from and inferior to scientific research, scholars have noted that Inuit knowledge can be regarded as comparable to science since, like science, it is "consensual, replicable, generalizable, incorporating, and to some extent experimental and predictive."[57] Kivalina's traditional knowledge, however, has not been granted the same level of authority as the master plan executed by the URS Corporation, and has been largely disregarded.

However, Kivalina also had scientific data supporting their traditional knowledge—specifically, studies by the National Oceanic and Atmospheric Administration (NOAA) suggesting Kiniktuuraq was actually accreting, not eroding, as downstream erosion from Kivalina was building up the site. After this information was presented to the Army Corps, Enoch Adams said, "We asked the Corps to do an audit of their information and they said they will and so far nothing has happened."[58] He was frustrated with the lack of response. "We're in the eleventh year of a five-year plan. If they had followed the original plans, we wouldn't have needed the seawall. We would be completely done this summer, according to their 1990s master schedule."

Patricia Opheen of the Army Corps said the NOAA study "does not delineate the floodplain" and "NOAA, from my knowledge, has never done a floodplain delineation, and if they were to do so it would need to be in coordination with FEMA, who oversees the delineation of floodplains for floodplain insurance."[59] The absence of such public data is a common problem for rural Alaska areas; in this case it leaves Kiniktuuraq ineligible for insurance and effectively makes government entities hesitant to allocate funds for construction in the area.

In its master plan URS went on to recommend Tatchim Isau as the preferred site, an area a few miles inland that Kivalina had not even put to a vote and many residents did not consider suitable for habitation. The recommendation was based on a variety of criteria, the main ones being storm-surge vulnerability, shoreline erosion vulnerability, water supply source and quality, community expansion potential, land status, and operation and maintenance costs.[60] The plan stated that Tatchim Isau was more cost-effective for relocation than Kiniktuuraq, since it was elevated and would not require gravel nourishment before construction, as the URS Corporation believed Kiniktuuraq did. Many Kivalina residents protested, arguing that inland areas have strong winds and are very cold, and make the costs of hunting very expensive due to their distance from bodies of water. Also, moving away from the coast would be a radical departure from Kivalina's traditional, subsistence way of life, tearing the people from their land and cultural fabric. As Enoch Adams said, "This area, it's part of us."[61]

Whalebone, sled, and boats, 2008

Disagreement over a new site has stalled an already painfully slow process, and is jeopardizing funding for not only relocation but also emergency assistance. Due to the high costs associated with construction in such remote areas, an evacuation road and evacuation site would ideally lead toward the new preferred location. Yet uncertainty over the new site has put the basic need for an evacuation road into question. According to Mike McKinnon of the Denali Commission, Denali considered building an evacuation road to Tatchim Isau, but then scrapped the plan as it became clear many Kivalina residents did not want to move there:

> Denali looked at an evacuation route from the community to higher territory, and found roads were between twenty and forty million dollars, and that was a rough estimate given hydrologic features we're trying to get past. It was decided that was too much money to spend on a road that would not be of use to Kivalina in the future. They wanted the road to go to a mountain that they could use for gravel to build up Kiniktuuraq. And that was a different purpose than Denali [had], which [was] to set up an evacuation site.[62]

This means that Kivalina has no evacuation road in the works.

When I spoke to tribal administrator Colleen Swan about the relocation, she sighed. Sitting at her desk in the city office, she looked emotionally exhausted, and it was clear that she has been dealing with the process for a very long time, with the weight of the village's future on her shoulders. She said,

> We don't have control over the relocation project or any project that the government pays for. It's just like, sometimes they're just going through the motions of consulting the tribe. Although they do find value in what we are able to contribute as the projects progress, because they need the local knowledge, but a lot of times we are butting heads because we don't make the final decision. The federal government has the money so they have the control. If they don't like the choice the people make, then the funding is not available.[63]

Enoch Adams noted the clear power dynamics involved in the process, which he situated within a broader timeline of historic injustice and inequality:

The federal government has a trust responsibility to the tribes, and they need to enact that. The state of Alaska needs to pony up monies that they have been taking by getting resources from our land, and share it with the communities that need it the most. When you take a real close look at this, this is a human rights issue. There is racism involved. There is class warfare. There is that rural versus urban Alaska thing. And when you really take a close look at those two designations, the urban areas are largely white, and rural largely native. This is a racial issue.[64]

When asked what might move the relocation process along, city administrator Janet Mitchell said, "Funding. That's the main factor. If we had funding, that would help considerably. And a lead entity," referring to an agency dedicated to relocation. Despite an acute awareness of what is needed, Kivalina has not been able to secure funding or agency support, even with all their efforts. "We pretty much have talked to everybody except the president of the United States," Janet said. "As much as we can, whenever we can, wherever we are, we mention the problems Kivalina is facing and that we need to relocate. We talked to [former Alaska] Governor Parnell, [former] Senator Stevens has been here and seen the problems we're facing. We've talked to the governor's office, FEMA, y'know, the Corps. Colleen [Swan] brings up the need for a lead entity at every meeting. Nothing happens."[65]

A 2009 GAO report echoed the feelings of Kivalina residents, aptly titled *Alaska Native Villages: Little Progress Has Been Made on Relocating Villages Threatened by Flooding and Erosion.*[66] As Kivalina has already known for two decades, the report identified an urgent need for a designated federal agency to help the village relocate. The report was then sent to government officials. When asked what would happen as a result, GAO senior analyst Allen Chan said government officials were positive about the report's call for a federal lead entity, but no definitive action was planned: "With the positive feedback there's been discus-

Kivalina, 2008

sions on the different possible ways that a lead entity could occur. There's interest in it. So at this point it seems very positive. But we haven't heard anything like, 'This is definitely going to happen now.' It's more like, they've asked us our opinions on what should happen, how should this be done."[67]

The GAO report also noted that another threatened village, New-tok, had chosen a new site and secured funding and assistance for an evacuation road to the site through the army's Innovative Readiness Training (IRT) program, designed to assist civil projects that serve as useful training exercises for the military. The program requires that the military's training needs are prioritized over the community's needs, as IRT shall "consist of activities essential to the accomplishment of military readiness training and offer incidental benefits to the community in which the training activities occur."[68] That only such restrictive assistance is available, placing public benefits secondary to military training goals, reinforces the need for programs that prioritize community safety above all else.

In August 2009, I phoned city administrator Janet Mitchell for an update. She sounded quite despondent. It was hard to hear her like that because, during my visit the previous year, Janet had been the most upbeat of the people I'd met. She knew the task ahead was difficult but seemed confident that it could be achieved—that the various projects and agencies could come together to make Kivalina's safe relocation possible. Such optimism was now completely stripped from her voice. When I asked what progress had been made on the relocation, she replied with a flat, "None." Indeed, in talking to her it became quite clear that, beyond completion of the funded portion of the rock revetment, little else had moved forward. Kivalina had requested that the data on Kiniktuuraq be reviewed but had heard no response. An evacuation road was still on hold. Without the support to move things forward, the informal plan is apparently to secure the village of Kivalina where it is, on an island that is eroding underneath its residents' feet.

This is the situation of Kivalina today. Fighting to be relocated, and hoping until then that their rock revetment proves resilient. Despite an-

Kivalina kids on all-terrain vehicle, 2008

cestry in the harsh Arctic going back thousands of years, this may prove the most difficult struggle yet for the people of Kivalina. And the world keeps warming, the ice keeps melting, and the storms keep coming.

CONCLUSION

Although climate change is often discussed as an environmental problem, its root causes are social. It stems from the fossilized carbon emissions we spew into our atmosphere and from the relations of power that make addressing this problem so difficult.

To maintain the use of fossil fuels, a small but influential group of companies and political and corporate supporters deliberately drew upon the PDI and its tactics to sow doubt about climate change and avoid regulatory action. In this attempt they have been all too successful; while awareness of their undermining efforts has grown, they have managed to create and sustain the illusion of a heated scientific debate for decades. To this day there are pockets of the U.S. population convinced that there is no problem, advocating the continued use of current energy sources without change or regulation.

As corporate and government officials refused to recognize or act on climate change, the Alaska Native village of Kivalina and a diverse group of lawyers filed a public nuisance lawsuit against fossil fuel companies. Kivalina's claim, however, was thrown out due to the political question doctrine: the court ruled that the issue of addressing climate change and its negative effects should be left to the very branches of government that had for so long ignored the issue, and even—during the George W. Bush administration—assisted in downplaying its severity.

Although the Kivalina ruling is being appealed and could be overturned, it is notable that the secondary claims of conspiracy and concert of action—focusing more directly on the fossil fuel industry's misinformation campaigns—were thrown out in these cases. Given the importance of such considerations in earlier suits against the asbestos and tobacco industries in determining the responsibility of those industries for the public harms caused by their products, the dismissal of these claims suggests that legal consideration of the damages caused by the misinformation campaigns of the fossil fuel industry may be far off. Further, although the dismissals of two other federal public nuisance claims were successfully appealed—*AEP* and *Comer*—the original *Comer* decision was reinstated soon afterward, and the Supreme Court has agreed to hear an appeal by the power company defendants in *AEP*, which could potentially affect all climate change lawsuits.

As the legal battle continues, Kivalina and other Alaska Natives affected by climate change are struggling to piece together their own relocation. And they are just a few among a growing number of communities whose lives are being disrupted by climate change.

The effects of climate change become more apparent every day. The year 2010 marked not just the hottest decade since instrumental climate records began in 1850—eighteen nations around the globe experienced their hottest temperatures ever—but also the wettest.[1] The IPCC notes that water vapor in the global atmosphere has increased by about 5 percent over the twentieth century, and 4 percent since 1970 alone. Although climate scientists are quick to note—accurately—that weather (short-term events) should not be conflated with climate (long-term conditions), it is also becoming clear that growing anthropogenic emissions are increasingly affecting the daily conditions of our lives, loading our atmosphere with more heat, precipitation, and energy in ways that can more readily lead to "extreme" weather events and disaster.

Meanwhile, fossil fuel companies and their supporters argue that the United States should continue drawing upon our oil, coal, and gas resources for our benefit. This argument, however, ignores that ownership of the resources and thus profits are concentrated among a small group of interests that are free to sell the resources as they see fit. This includes the steady exporting of "our" coal, even as coal companies argue the United States should not lower limits on greenhouse gas emissions until developing nations lower theirs. Despite not owning the resources, the public pays the costs: in the United States, fossil fuel companies enjoy tax breaks, government-backed loans, grants, the public subsidizing of the negative environmental and health effects, and funding for overseas military operations that safeguard oil supplies and trading.

The additional costs of fossil fuels also became apparent in April 2010, with the Massey coal mine explosion that killed twenty-nine, and the BP Deepwater Horizon oil rig explosion that killed eleven and resulted in the largest oil spill in U.S. history. Similar disasters, meanwhile, are all too common throughout the rest of the world, including frequent coal mining "accidents" in China, widespread population displacement for the construction of coal mines and plants in countries such as Burma and Thailand, and oil "spills" that have long plagued Ecuador and Nigeria. These kinds of events will become more frequent as current fossil fuel supplies deplete and companies pursue harder-to-reach sources with more unconventional techniques, such as offshore oil drilling in the remote Arctic, blasting water and chemicals into the.

Marcellus Shale underlying the northeastern United States, and pumping increasing amounts of captured carbon dioxide underground for enhanced oil recovery.

Fossil fuels are not the only option, however, and the science on climate change suggests that what's left of them should be used wisely, moving toward a model of smaller and more local development powered by cleaner energy sources. Despite a widespread perception in the United States that renewable energy sources such as wind, solar, and geothermal are not feasible as long-term alternatives, they are already successfully deployed throughout the world. They are also a high-growth sector: a 2010 Pew report found that, from 1998 to 2007, U.S. jobs in the green energy sector grew 2.5 times faster than jobs overall.[2] These jobs are growing despite uneven U.S. government policies and support: research and development (R&D) funds and financial incentives for renewables are often trimmed or not renewed, creating an unstable and unpredictable market for their full implementation.

History suggests technologies do not develop in a vacuum, and often involve both the private and public sector: microchips, semiconductors, jet engines, personal computers, and the Internet all became high-growth industries in the United States through government R&D and support.[3] Stronger investments in green energy technologies, combined with increases in energy efficiency and conservation, can help mitigate warming and create new market sectors, as well as provide revenues to assist those who are and will be affected by climate change.

As this book has argued, climate change is a social issue that increasingly affects all of us. The dangers have become clear, imperiling people throughout the world like those in Kivalina, and it is time to act. To fail to do so is to leave this issue to the small number of powerful players who exert so much influence over U.S. and global policy, many of whom have worked very hard to dispute and downplay climate change and block meaningful action. We cannot afford to leave the fate of our planet in their hands. It is up to all of us.

NOTES

Introduction

1. Weart, *The Discovery of Global Warming*.
2. Petit, et al. "Climate and Atmospheric History of the Past 420,000 Years from the Vostok Ice Core, Antarctica."
3. Hansen, *Storms of My Grandchildren*.
4. Kintisch, "Global Warming: Projections of Climate Change Go from Bad to Worse."
5. Hansen, *Storms of My Grandchildren*.

Chapter One: Blueprint for Denial

1. Associated Press, "Science Not Faked But Not Pretty."
2. Freudenburg, Gramling, and Davidson, "Scientific Certainty Argumentation Methods (SCAMs)."
3. Oreskes, "Science and Public Policy."
4. Michaels, *Doubt Is Their Product*.
5. Phillips, *American Theocracy*; Phillips, *American Dynasty*.
6. Bowker, *Fatal Deception*.
7. Markowitz and Rosner, "The Limits of Thresholds."
8. Scott, *Muscle and Blood*.
9. Rampton and Stauber, *Trust Us, We're Experts!*
10. Markowitz and Rosner, "The Limits of Thresholds"; McCulloch and Tweedale, *Defending the Indefensible*.
11. Markowitz and Rosner, "The Limits of Thresholds."
12. Ibid.
13. Interview by author, March 18, 2009.
14. Michaels, *Doubt Is Their Product*; Freudenburg, Gramling, and Davidson, "Scientific

Certainty Argumentation Methods (SCAMs)."
15. Castleman, *Asbestos: Medical and Legal Aspects.*
16. McCulloch and Tweedale, *Defending the Indefensible.*
17. Bowker, *Fatal Deception.*
18. Michaels, *Doubt Is Their Product.*
19. Miller, *The Voice of Business.*
20. Michaels, *Doubt Is Their Product.*
21. Interview by author, March 25, 2009.
22. Freudenburg, Gramling, and Davidson, "Scientific Certainty Argumentation Methods (SCAMs)."
23. McCulloch and Tweedale, *Defending the Indefensible.*
24. Markowitz and Rosner, "Cater to the Children."
25. Ibid.
26. Ibid.
27. Michaels, *Doubt Is Their Product.*
28. Perillo, "Scraping beneath the Surface."
29. Markowitz and Rosner, "Cater to the Children."
30. Rosner and Markowitz, "A 'Gift of God'?: The Public Health Controversy over Leaded Gasoline during the 1920s."
31. Denworth, *Toxic Truth.*
32. Ibid.
33. Kraft and Scheberle, "Environmental Justice and the Allocation of Risk."
34. Interview by author, March 19, 2009.
35. Kluger, *Ashes to Ashes.*
36. Glantz, *The Cigarette Papers.*
37. Michaels, *Doubt Is Their Product*; Fritschler, *Tobacco and Politics.*
38. Miller, *The Voice of Business.*
39. Kluger, *Ashes to Ashes.*
40. Glantz, *The Cigarette Papers.*
41. Ibid.
42. Diehl, *Tobacco & Your Health.*
43. Kluger, *Ashes to Ashes.*
44. Michaels, *Doubt Is Their Product.*
45. Glantz, *The Cigarette Papers.*
46. Guardino and Daynard, "Tobacco Industry Lawyers as 'Disease Vectors.'"
47. Zimring, "Comparing Cigarette Policy and Illicit Drug and Alcohol Control."
48. Mooney, *Republican War on Science.*
49. Glantz, *The Cigarette Papers.*
50. Mooney, *Republican War on Science.*
51. Monbiot, *Heat.*
52. Mooney, *Republican War on Science.*
53. MacCleery, *Safeguards at Risk.*
54. Phillips, *American Theocracy.*

55. Mooney, *Republican War on Science.*
56. Sanjour, *Why EPA Is Like It Is and What Can Be Done about It.*
57. Ibid.
58. Kennedy, *Crimes against Nature.*
59. Freudenburg and Gramling, "Bureaucratic Slippage and Failures of Agency Vigilance."
60. Kennedy, *Crimes against Nature.*
61. Oreskes, "Science and Public Policy"; Mooney, *Republican War on Science.*
62. Freudenburg, "Privileged Access, Privileged Accounts."
63. Costanza, et al., "The Value of the World's Ecosystem Services and Natural Capital."
64. Rich and Weaver, "Think Tanks in the U.S. Media."
65. Jacques, Dunlap, and Freeman, "The Organisation of Denial."

Chapter Two: Shaping Legality

1. Reichman, "Moving Backstage"; Snider, "Sociology of Corporate Crime."
2. Koenig and Rustad, "Crimtorts as Corporate Just Deserts"; Koenig and Rustad, *Toxic Torts, Politics, and Environmental Justice*; Koenig, "Crimtorts: A Cure for Hardening of the Categories."
3. Ewick and Silbey, "Conformity, Contestation, and Resistance."
4. Freudenburg, "Privileged Access, Privileged Accounts."
5. Simons, "The Crime/Tort Distinction: Legal Doctrine and Normative Perspectives."
6. Koenig, "Crimtorts: A Cure for Hardening of the Categories."
7. Schwartz and Goldberg, "The Law of Public Nuisance: Maintaining Rational Boundaries on a Rational Tort."
8. Rosen, "'Knowing' Industrial Pollution."
9. Ibid.
10. Galanter, *Tournament of Lawyers.*
11. Lipartito and Pratt, *Baker & Botts in the Development of Modern Houston.*
12. Janutis, "The Struggle over Tort Reform and the Overlooked Legacy of the Progressives."
13. Grossman and Adams, *Taking Care of Business*; Nace, *Gangs of America*; Hartmann, *Unequal Protection*; O'Brien, *Storm Center*; Magrath, *Morrison R. Waite.*
14. Grossman and Adams, *Taking Care of Business.*
15. Wells, *Corporations and Criminal Responsibility.*
16. Castleman, *Asbestos: Medical and Legal Aspects.*
17. Brodeur, *Outrageous Misconduct.*
18. Selikoff, Churg, and Hammond, "Relation between Exposure to Asbestos and Mesothelioma."
19. McCulloch and Tweedale, *Defending the Indefensible.*
20. Ibid.
21. Carroll, *Asbestos Litigation.*
22. McCulloch and Tweedale, *Defending the Indefensible.*
23. Ibid.
24. Kelder and Daynard, *Judicial Approaches to Tobacco Control.*

25. Nader and Smith, *No Contest.*
26. *Haines v. Liggett Group,* 1993: 421.
27. Nader and Smith, *No Contest.*
28. Mather, "Theorizing about Trial Courts."
29. Daynard, *Tobacco Liability Litigation as a Cancer Control Strategy.*
30. Galanter, *Why the Haves Come out Ahead.*
31. Mollenkamp, *The People vs. Big Tobacco.*
32. Stone, "Grassroots Group Rakes in the Green."
33. Reynolds, "Tort Reform Project."
34. Silverstein, *The Tobacco Industry's Influence on the Phony 'Grassroots' Campaign for Liability Limits.*
35. Friedman, "Tobacco Industry Use of Judicial Seminars."
36. Ibid.
37. Mercer and Edmond, "Daubert and the Exclusionary Ethos."
38. Friedman, "Tobacco Industry Use of Judicial Seminars."
39. Friedman, Daynard, and Banthin, "How Tobacco-Friendly Science Escapes Scrutiny in the Courtroom."
40. Zernike, "Secretive Republican Donors Are Planning Ahead."
41. Mayer, "Covert Operations."
42. Kraft and Scheberle, "Environmental Justice and the Allocation of Risk"; Rabin, "The Rhode Island Lead Paint Lawsuit."
43. Kraft and Scheberle, "Environmental Justice and the Allocation of Risk."
44. Rabin, "The Rhode Island Lead Paint Lawsuit."
45. Mank, "Standing and Global Warming."
46. Tipps, "Why Control Is Not an Element of Public Nuisance"; Keeton, *Prosser and Keeton on the Law of Torts.*
47. Gifford, "Public Nuisance as a Mass Products Liability Tort."
48. Schwartz and Goldberg, "The Law of Public Nuisance."
49. *In Re Lead Paint Litigation* 924 A.2d, 440, quoting *Camden County Bd. of Chosen Free-holders v. Beretta, U.S.A. Corp* (3d Cir. 2001), 540.
50. Ibid., 425, 429.
51. *State of R.I. v. Lead Industries Association* 951 A.2d, 449, quoting Gifford, "Public Nuisance as a Mass Products Liability Tort," 820.
52. Ibid., 450, quoting Schwartz and Goldberg, "The Law of Public Nuisance," 568.
53. Ibid., 449; Gagliardi, "Stirring the Debate in Rhode Island."
54. Interview by author, May 28, 2009.
55. Interview by author, May 27, 2009.
56. LexisNexis, *The Rhode Island Lead Lawsuit.*

Chapter Three: Fossil Fuels and U.S. Power

1. Energy Information Administration, "Greenhouse Gases, Climate Change, and Energy."
2. Freudenburg and Gramling, *Oil in Troubled Waters*; Larsen and Shah, *World Fossil*

Fuel Subsidies and Global Carbon Emissions.

3. Environmental Protection Agency, "Executive Summary: 2009 U.S. Greenhouse Inventory Report."
4. Energy Information Administration, "Major U.S. Coal Producers, 2008."
5. Goodell, *Big Coal.*
6. Energy Information Administration, "Major U.S. Coal Producers, 2008."
7. Freudenburg, " Privileged Access, Privileged Accounts."
8. Reardon, "Private Equity Firms and the Irrelevance of Traditional Monopoly."
9. Goodell, *Big Coal*; Kazis and Grossman, *Fear at Work.*
10. Derickson, *Black Lung.*
11. Weeks, "Tampering with Dust Samples in Coal Mines (Again)"; Cook, "Coal Miners Slaughter."
12. Auty, *Sustaining Development in Mineral Economies.*
13. Frank, *The Development of Underdevelopment.*
14. Freudenburg and Wilson, "Mining the Data."
15. Goodell, *Big Coal.*
16. Templet, "Grazing the Commons."
17. Erikson, "Disaster at Buffalo Creek."
18. Hansen and Janes, *Coal Mining and the Clean Water Act.*
19. Duhigg, "Cleansing the Air at the Expense of Waterways."
20. Turka and Gray, "Impacts of Coal Mining."
21. Environmental Protection Agency, "Executive Summary: 2009 U.S. Greenhouse Inventory Report."
22. Goodell, *Big Coal.*
23. Wickham, et al., "The Effect of Appalachian Mountaintop Mining."
24. Environmental Protection Agency, *Mountaintop Mining/Valley Fills in Appalachia.*
25. Nace, "Climate Hope."
26. Wilkinson, "Home Dance, the Hopi, and Black Mesa Coal"; Cole and Foster, *From the Ground Up.*
27. Cole and Foster, *From the Ground Up.*
28. Churchill, *Struggle for the Land.*
29. Gedicks, *Resource Rebels.*
30. Chandler, "The Beginnings of Big Business in American Industry."
31. Kelley, *Energy in America.*
32. Rudolph and Ridley, *Power Struggle.*
33. Novick, "The Electric Power Industry."
34. Beder, *Power Play.*
35. Kelley, *Energy in America*; Rudolph and Ridley, *Power Struggle.*
36. Beder, *Power Play.*
37. Hirsch, *Power Loss.*
38. Johnson, *The Politics of Soft Coal.*
39. Rudolph and Ridley, *Power Struggle.*
40. Beder, *Power Play.*

41. Lipartito and Pratt, *Baker & Botts in the Development of Modern Houston*.
42. Thompson, *Confessions of the Power Trust*.
43. Lipartito and Pratt, *Baker & Botts in the Development of Modern Houston*.
44. McDonald, *Insull*.
45. Rudolph and Ridley, *Power Struggle*.
46. Beder, *Power Play*.
47. Rudolph and Ridley, *Power Struggle*.
48. Ibid.
49. Phillips, *American Dynasty*; Partnoy, *Infectious Greed: How Deceit and Risk Corrupted the Financial Markets*; Gibney, et al., *Enron: The Smartest Guys in the Room*.
50. Beder, *Power Play*.
51. Fusaro and Wilcox, *Energy Derivatives*.
52. Gibney, et al., *Enron: The Smartest Guys in the Room*.
53. Partnoy, *Infectious Greed*.
54. Beder, *Power Play*.
55. Gibney, et al., *Enron: The Smartest Guys in the Room*; Blackburn, "The Enron Debacle and the Pension Crisis."
56. Environmental Information Agency, *The Changing Structure of the Electric Power Industry 2000: An Update*.
57. Beder, *Power Play*.
58. Davis, "Morgan Stanley Trades Energy Old-fashioned Way."
59. Senate Committee on Homeland Security and Governmental Affairs, "The Role of Market Speculation in Rising Oil and Gas Prices."
60. Fusaro and Vasey, *Energy and Environmental Hedge Funds*.
61. Juhasz, *The Tyranny of Oil*; Taibbi, "The Great American Bubble Machine."
62. Goodell, *Big Coal*.
63. Ibid.
64. Epstein, et al., "Full Cost Accounting for the Life Cycle of Coal."
65. Kubasek and Silverman, *Environmental Law*.
66. Kelley, *Energy in America*.
67. Fox, *Gasland*.
68. Kelley, *Energy in America*.
69. Environmental Information Agency, *U.S. Coal Exports: Data for October–December (4th Quarter 2009)*.
70. Beder, *Power Play*; Stiglitz, *Globalization and Its Discontents*.
71. Government Accountability Office, "Coal Power Plants."
72. Fisher, "Bringing the Material Back In."
73. Doyle and Risely, *Crucible for Survival*.
74. Kelley, *Energy in America*.
75. Little, *Power Trip*.
76. Tarbell, *The History of the Standard Oil Company*.
77. Ibid.
78. Juhasz, *The Tyranny of Oil*.

79. Yergin, *The Prize*.
80. Juhasz, *The Tyranny of Oil*.
81. Zinn, *A People's History of the United States*.
82. Juhasz, *The Tyranny of Oil*.
83. Ibid.
84. Ibid.
85. Tickell, Murphy, and Graziano, *Biodiesel America*.
86. Adler, "The Transformation of the Pacific Electric Railway."
87. Phillips, *American Theocracy*.
88. Yergin, *The Prize*; Lauman and Knoke, *The Organizational State*.
89. Phillips, *American Theocracy*.
90. Odell, *Oil and World Power*.
91. Juhasz, *The Tyranny of Oil*.
92. Sampson, *The Seven Sisters*.
93. Klare, *Blood and Oil*.
94. Phillips, *American Dynasty*.
95. Jarecki, *Why We Fight*.
96. Stiglitz, *Globalization and its Discontents*.
97. Freudenburg and Gramling, *Oil in Troubled Waters*; Klare, *Blood and Oil*.
98. Johnson, *Blowback*.
99. Hardt and Negri, *Empire*.
100. Klare, *Blood and Oil*.
101. Freudenburg and Gramling, *Oil in Troubled Waters*.
102. Little, *Power Trip*.
103. Leggett, *Half Gone*.
104. Ibid.
105. Klare, *Blood and Oil*.
106. Campbell and Laherrere, "The End of Cheap Oil"; Deffeyes, *Hubbert's Peak*.
107. Leggett, *Half Gone*.
108. Molotch, "Oil in Santa Barbara and Power in America."
109. Kubasek and Silverman, *Environmental Law*; Epstein and Selber, *Oil: A Life Cycle Analysis of Its Health and Environmental Impacts*; Epstein, Greetham, and Karuba, *Ranking Refineries*; Beamish, "Waiting for Crisis."
110. Roddick, *The Dance of the Millions*.
111. Phillips, *American Theocracy*.
112. Unger, *House of Bush, House of Saud*.
113. Juhasz, *The Tyranny of Oil*.
114. Bradsher, *High and Mighty*.
115. Juhasz, *The Tyranny of Oil*.
116. Ibid.
117. Phillips, *American Theocracy*.
118. Juhasz, *The Tyranny of Oil*.
119. Ibid.

120. Phillips, *American Theocracy*.
121. Phillips, *American Dynasty*.
122. Phillips, *American Theocracy*.
123. Ibid.
124. Gellman, *Angler: The Cheney Vice Presidency*.
125. Ibid.
126. Phillips, *American Dynasty*.
127. Dickinson, "Obama's Sheriff."
128. Ibid.
129. Monbiot, *Heat*.
130. Dickinson, "Obama's Sheriff."
131. Klare, *Blood and Oil*.
132. Phillips, *American Dynasty*.
133. Scahill, *Blackwater*.
134. Klein, *The Shock Doctrine*.
135. Kramer, "Deals with Iraq Are Set to Bring Oil Giants Back."
136. Juhasz, *The Tyranny of Oil*.

Chapter Four: Global What?

1.   Pachauri and Reisinger, *Climate Change 2007*.
2.   Fleming, *Historical Perspectives on Climate Change*.
3.   Weart, *The Discovery of Global Warming*.
4.   Fleming, *Historical Perspectives on Climate Change*.
5.   Pace and Groffman, *Successes, Limitations, and Frontiers in Ecosystem Science*.
6.   Weart, *The Discovery of Global Warming*.
7.   Rodhe, Charlson, and Crawford, "Svante Arrhenius and the Greenhouse Effect"; Pachauri and Reisinger, *Climate Change 2007*.
8.   Weart, *The Discovery of Global Warming*.
9.   Johnson, *Investigating Climate Change*.
10. Bowen, *Thin Ice*.
11. Ibid.
12. Mooney, *Storm World*.
13. Redfield, "The Biological Control of Chemical Factors in the Environment."
14. Weart, *The Discovery of Global Warming*.; Helvarg, *Blue Frontier*.
15. Henson, *The Rough Guide to Climate Change*.
16. Weart, *The Discovery of Global Warming*.
17. Broecker and Kunzig, *Fixing Climate*.
18. Bolin and Eriksson, "Changes in the Carbon Dioxide Content of the Atmosphere and Sea Due to Fossil Fuel Combustion."
19. Weart, *The Discovery of Global Warming*.
20. Flannery, *The Weather Makers*.
21. Weart, *The Discovery of Global Warming*.

22. Pearce, *With Speed and Violence.*
23. Bowen, *Thin Ice.*
24. Weart, *The Discovery of Global Warming.*
25. Pachauri and Reisinger, *Climate Change 2007.*
26. CO2now.org, "Current Data for Atmospheric CO2."
27. Hansen, et al., "Climate Impact of Increasing Atmospheric Carbon Dioxide."
28. Weart, *The Discovery of Global Warming.*
29. Mooney, *Republican War on Science*; Oreskes, Conway, and Shindell, "From Chicken Little to Dr. Pangloss."
30. Houghton, Jenkins, and Ephraums, *Executive Summary on Climate Change for Policymakers.*
31. IPCC, "The Science of Climate Change."
32. Oreskes, *Beyond the Ivory Tower.*
33. Flannery, *The Weather Makers.*
34. Weart, *The Discovery of Global Warming.*
35. Mooney, *Storm World.*
36. Weart, *The Discovery of Global Warming*; Pachauri and Reisinger, *Climate Change 2007*; Flannery, *The Weather Makers*; Dumanoski, *The End of the Long Summer*; Hansen, *Storms of My Grandchildren.*
37. Weart, *The Discovery of Global Warming.*
38. Pachauri and Reisinger, *Climate Change 2007.*
39. Mooney, *Storm World.*
40 MSNBC, "Nixon Administration Debated Global Warming."
41. Oreskes, Conway, and Shindell, "From Chicken Little to Dr. Pangloss."
42. Mooney, *Republican War on Science.*
43. Gelbspan, *The Heat Is On.*
44. Ibid.
45. Ibid.
46. Monbiot, *Heat.*
47. Ibid.
48. Gelbspan, *The Heat Is On.*
49. Monbiot, *Heat.*
50. Mooney, *Republican War on Science*; Gelbspan, *The Heat Is On.*
51. Boykoff and Boykoff, "Bias as Balance"; Corbett and Durfee, "Testing Public (un)Certainty of Science."
52. Flannery, *The Weather Makers.*
53. Monbiot, *Heat.*
54. Flannery, *The Weather Makers.*
55. Ibid.
56. Gelbspan, *The Heat Is On.*
57. Leggett, *Half Gone.*
58. Leggett, *Half Gone*; Leggett, *The Carbon War*; Newell, *Climate for Change.*
59. Newell, *Climate for Change.*

60. Roberts, "Global Inequality and Climate Change."
61. McCright and Dunlap, "Challenging Global Warming as a Social Problem"; McCright and Dunlap, "Defeating Kyoto."
62. Krosnick, Holbrook, and Visser, "The Impact of the Fall 1997 Debate"; Lorenzoni, Pidgeon, and O'Connor, "Dangerous Climate Change."
63. Hamilton, *Scorcher.*
64. Vidal, "Revealed: How Oil Giant Influenced Bush."
65. Monbiot, *Heat.*
66. Mooney, *Republican War on Science.*
67. Cushman, "Industrial Group Plans to Battle Climate Treaty."
68. Ibid.
69. Ibid.
70. Union of Concerned Scientists, "Smoke, Mirrors, and Hot Air."
71. Greenpeace, *Koch Industries.*
72. Michaels, *Doubt Is Their Product*; Mooney, *Republican War on Science.*
73. Monbiot, *Heat.*
74. Michaels, *Doubt Is Their Product.*
75. Center for Responsive Politics, "James M. Inhofe: Industry Data."
76. Mooney, *Republican War on Science.*
77. Michaels, *Doubt Is Their Product*; Mooney, *Republican War on Science.*
78. Michaels, *Doubt Is Their Product.*
79. Mooney, *Storm World.*
80. Michaels, *Doubt Is Their Product*; Mooney, *Storm World.*
81. Donaghy, et al., "Atmosphere of Pressure."
82. Michaels, *Doubt Is Their Product.*
83. Weart, *The Discovery of Global Warming*; Pachauri and Reisinger, *Climate Change 2007*; Flannery, *The Weather Makers*; Pearce, *With Speed and Violence.*
84. Mooney, *Storm World.*
85. Revkin, "Industry Ignored Its Scientists on Climate."
86. Ibid.
87. Denial of Petition to Regulate GHGs. Fed. Reg. 68 (2008) p. 52925.
88. Ibid., 52925–30.
89. Ibid., 52925.
90. Mass. v. EPA, 415 F. 3d 2005.
91. Mass. v. EPA, U.S. 2007.
92. Schaeffer, "Junketing Judges."
93. Zinn, *A People's History of the United States.*
94. Baker v. Carr, 369 U.S. 186, 217.
95. Ibid.
96. Cole and Foster, *From the Ground Up.*
97. Connecticut v. AEP, 406 F. Supp. 2d, 271.
98. Ibid., 273–4.
99. Ibid., 280; Silbey and Bittner, "The Availability of Law."

100. Mass. v. EPA, U.S. 2007.
101. CA v. GM, WL 2726871, *14, quoting *EPA* in 68 Fed. Reg. at 52927, 52931.
102. Comer v. Murphy Oil Co. S.D. Miss. (August 30, 2007).
103. Goodell, "Secretary of Saving the Planet."
104. Freudenburg, Gramling, and Davidson, "Scientific Certainty Argumentation Methods (SCAMs)"; Auyero and Swistun, "The Social Production of Toxic Uncertainty"; Proctor and Fox, "Cancer Wars."
105. Oreskes, Conway, and Shindell, "From Chicken Little to Dr. Pangloss."
106. McCright and Dunlap, "Defeating Kyoto"; Freudenburg, "Social Constructions and Social Constrictions."

Chapter Five: The Human Face of Global Warming

1. Cole and Foster, *From the Ground Up.*
2. Annan and Stocking, *Climate Change.*
3. O'Neill, *Last Giant of Beringia.*
4. Borneman, *Alaska: Saga of a Bold Land.*
5. Ibid.
6. Chance, *The Iñupiat and Arctic Alaska.*
7. Ibid.
8. Borneman, *Alaska: Saga of a Bold Land.*
9. Case and Dorough, "Tribes and Self-Determination in Alaska."
10. Ibid.
11. Haycox, *Alaska: An American Colony.*
12. Ibid.
13. Spring, *The Cultural Transformation.*
14. Chance, *The Iñupiat and Arctic Alaska*; Burch, "The Inupiat and the Christianization of Arctic Alaska."
15. Burch, *Social Life in Northwest Alaska.*
16. Brown, "Political and Legal Status of Alaska Natives."
17. Chance, "Modernization and Educational Reform in Native Alaska."
18. Chance, *The Iñupiat and Arctic Alaska.*
19. O'Neill, "Frozen in Time."
20. Olson, *The Struggle for the Land.*
21. Haycox, *Alaska: An American Colony.*
22. Standlea, *Oil, Globalization, and the War for the Arctic Refuge.*
23. O'Neill, *The Firecracker Boys*; Brown, "Political and Legal Status of Alaska Natives."
24. Olthuis, *It Happened in Alaska.*
25. Wilkinson, *Blood Struggle.*
26. Redmond, *The New Horizon.*
27. Leggett, *Half Gone*; Chance, *The Iñupiat and Arctic Alaska.*
28. Haycox, *Alaska: An American Colony.*
29. Wilkinson, *Blood Struggle.*
30. Olson, *The Struggle for the Land.*

31. Chance, *The Iñupiat and Arctic Alaska.*
32. Olthuis, *It Happened in Alaska*; Redmond, *The New Horizon.*
33. Chance, *The Iñupiat and Arctic Alaska.*
34. Brown, "Political and Legal Status of Alaska Natives."
35. Ibid.
36. Standlea, *Oil, Globalization, and the War for the Arctic Refuge.*
37. Cronon and Miles, *Under an Open Sky.*
38. Strohmeyer, *Extreme Conditions: Big Oil and the Transformation of Alaska*; Gramling and Freudenburg, "The Exxon Valdez Oil Spill in the Context of US Petroleum Politics."
39. Government Accountability Office, *Alaska Native Villages.*
40. Berardi, "Natural Resource Policy, Unforgiving Geographies, and Persistent Poverty in Alaska Native Villages."
41. Edwards and Natarajan, "ANCSA and ANILCA: Capabilities Failure?"
42. Berardi, "Natural Resource Policy, Unforgiving Geographies, and Persistent Poverty in Alaska Native Villages."
43. Edwards and Natarajan, "ANCSA and ANILCA: Capabilities Failure?"
44. Brown, "Political and Legal Status of Alaska Natives."
45. Berardi, "Natural Resource Policy, Unforgiving Geographies, and Persistent Poverty in Alaska Native Villages."
46. Brown, "Political and Legal Status of Alaska Natives."
47. Bullard, *Confronting Environmental Racism: Voices from the Grassroots*; Checker, *Polluted Promises.*
48. Commission for Racial Justice, *Toxic Wastes and Race in the U.S.*; Mohai and Bryant, *Environmental Racism: Reviewing the Evidence.*
49. Cole and Foster, *From the Ground Up.*
50. Ibid.; Bullard, *Confronting Environmental Racism*; Checker, *Polluted Promises.*
51. Cole and Foster, *From the Ground Up.*
52. Interview by author, August 26, 2008.
53. Ibid.
54. National Assessment Synthesis Team, *Climate Change Impacts on the United States.*
55. Ibid.
56. Government Accountability Office, *Alaska Native Villages: Most Are Affected by Flooding and Erosion.*
57. Gordon, "Inter-American Commission on Human Rights to Hold Hearing."
58. U.S. Army Corps of Engineers, *Alaska Village Erosion Technical Assistance Program.*
59. Government Accountability Office, *Alaska Native Villages: Limited Progress Has Been Made*; GAO, *Alaska Native Villages: Most Are Affected by Flooding and Erosion*; U.S. Army Corps of Engineers, *Kivalina Relocation Master Plan.*
60. Interview by author, July 25, 2008.
61. Interview by author, August 26, 2008.
62. Interview by author, August 18, 2009.
63. Interview by author, July 25, 2008.
64. Interview by author, May 2, 2009.

65. Ibid.
66. Mollenkamp, *The People vs. Big Tobacco*
67. Interview by author, August 4, 2009.
68. Ibid.
69. Klein, "James Baker's Double Life."
70. Unger, *House of Bush, House of Saud.*
71. Mooney, *Republican War on Science*; Silverstein, *The Tobacco Industry's Influence on the Phony 'Grassroots' Campaign for Liability Limits*; Covington and Burling, *Tort Reform Project Budget.*
72. Sample, "Scientists Offered Cash to Dispute Climate Study."
73. MacCleery, *Safeguards at Risk*; Kennedy, *Crimes against Nature.*
74. Connecticut vs. AEP, WL 2996729 (2009).
75. Ibid., 22.
76. Ibid., 34, emphasis theirs.
77. Native Village of Kivalina v. ExxonMobil Corp. C 08-1138 SBA, 12 (N.D. Cal. 2009), 12.
78. Comer v. Murphy Oil Co. WL 3321493 (2009).
79. Ibid., 16.
80. Ibid., 29.
81. Ibid., 29.
82. Freudenburg, et al., *Catastrophe in the Making.*
83. Interview by author, August 3, 2009.

Chapter Six: Relocation in a Neoliberal State

1. Darlington, "Kivalina, Alaska: A Melting Village."
2. Interview by author, August 8, 2008.
3. Gray, *Situation Assessment.*
4. Tierney, Lindell, and Perry, *Facing the Unexpected.*
5. Gramling and Freudenburg, "The Exxon Valdez Oil Spill in the Context of US Petroleum Politics"; Hirt, *A Conspiracy of Optimism*; Helvarg, *Blue Frontier*; Freudenburg, et al., *Catastrophe in the Making.*
6. Lavell, "Decision Making and Risk Management"; Hansen and Oliver-Smith, *Involuntary Migration and Resettlement*; Hewitt, *Interpretations of Calamity.*
7. Osborne, *The History of Military Assistance.*
8. Cooper and Block, *Disaster: Hurricane Katrina and the Failure of Homeland Security.*
9. Ibid.
10. Ibid.
11. Tierney, *Disaster Beliefs and Institutional Interests*; Cooper and Block, *Disaster: Hurricane Katrina and the Failure of Homeland Security.*
12. Scahill, *Blackwater.*
13. Wenger, et al., "It's a Matter of Myths"; Fischer, *Response to Disaster*; Solnit, *A Paradise Built in Hell.*
14. Tierney, "Disaster Beliefs and Institutional Interests."

15. Tierney, Lindell, and Perry, *Facing the Unexpected*; Solnit, *A Paradise Built in Hell*.
16. Freudenburg, et al., *Catastrophe in the Making*.
17. Scahill, *Blackwater*.
18. Ibid.
19. Freudenburg, et al., *Catastrophe in the Making*; Solnit, *A Paradise Built in Hell*; Clarke, "Considering Katrina."
20. Klein, *The Shock Doctrine*; Gotham and Greenberg, "From 9/11 to 8/29."
21. Steinberg, *Acts of God*.
22. Interview by author, August 8, 2009.
23. Mitchell, "Erosion."
24. Scherer, "Little Big Companies."
25. Ibid.
26. Wallace-Wells, "Polar Fleeced."
27. Mitchell, "Erosion."
28. Interview by author, August 9, 2009.
29. Interview by author, August 7, 2008.
30. U.S. Army Corps of Engineers, *Environmental Assessment*.
31. Ibid.
32. Interview by author, August 8, 2008.
33. Interview by author, August 8, 2008.
34. Interview by author, August 11, 2008.
35. Interview by author, August 9, 2008.
36. Interview by author, August 9, 2008.
37. Interview by author, September 4, 2009.
38. U.S. Army Corps of Engineers, *Environmental Assessment*.
39. Government Accountability Office, *Alaska Native Villages: Limited Progress Has Been Made*.
40. Interview by author, August 8, 2008.
41. Interview by author, August 9, 2008.
42. Interview by author, August 9, 2008.
43. Interview by author, August 7, 2008.
44. Interview by author, August 8, 2008.
45. Cooper and Block, *Disaster: Hurricane Katrina and the Failure of Homeland Security*.
46. Government Accountability Office, *Alaska Native Villages: Limited Progress Has Been Made*.
47. Interview by author, August 20, 2009.
48. Pinter, "One Step Forward, Two Steps Back on U.S. Floodplains."
49. Patricia Opheen, interview by author, September 4, 2009.
50. Cooper and Block, *Disaster: Hurricane Katrina and the Failure of Homeland Security*.
51. Mitchell, "Relocation."
52. Ibid.
53. U.S. Army Corps of Engineers, *Kivalina Relocation Master Plan*, 77.
54. Interview by author, August 8, 2008.

55. Interview by author, August 8, 2008.
56. Agrawal, "Dismantling the Divide between Indigenous and Scientific Knowledge."
57. Ibid.
58. Interview by author, August 8, 2008.
59. Interview by author, September 4, 2009.
60. U.S. Army Corps of Engineers, *Kivalina Relocation Master Plan.*.
61. Interview by author, August 8, 2008.
62. Interview by author, August 20, 2009.
63. Interview by author, August 7, 2008.
64. Interview by author, August 8, 2008.
65. Interview by author, August 25, 2008.
66. Government Accountability Office, *Alaska Native Villages: Limited Progress Has Been Made.*
67. Interview by author, July 28, 2009.
68. Office of the Assistant Secretary of Defense for Reserve Affairs, *Support and Services for Eligible Organizations.*

Conclusion

1. National Oceanic and Atmospheric Administration, "2011 Tied for Warmest Year on Record."
2. Pew Charitable Trust, *Who's Winning the Clean Energy Race?*
3. Breakthrough Institute, *Case Studies in American Innovation.*

BIBLIOGRAPHY

References

Adler, Sy. "The Transformation of the Pacific Electric Railway: Bradford Snell, Roger Rabbit, and the Politics of Transportation in Los Angeles." *Urban Affairs Quarterly* 27, no. 1 (1991): 51–86.

Agrawal, Arun. "Dismantling the Divide between Indigenous and Scientific Knowledge." *Development and Change* 26, no. 3 (1995): 413–439.

Andrews, Richard N. L. *Managing the Environment, Managing Ourselves: A History of American Environmental Policy.* New Haven, CT: Yale University Press, 2006.

Annan, Kofi and Barbara Stocking. *Human Impact Report: Climate Change—the Anatomy of a Silent Crisis.* Geneva, Switzerland: Global Humanitarian Forum, 2009.

Associated Press. "Science Not Faked But Not Pretty." December 8, 2009.

Auty, Richard M. *Sustaining Development in Mineral Economies: The Resource Curse Thesis.* New York: Routledge, 1993.

Auyero, Javier and Debora Swistun. "The Social Production of Toxic Uncertainty." *American Sociological Review* 73, no. 3 (2008): 357.

Beamish, Thomas D. "Waiting for Crisis: Regulatory Inaction and Ineptitude and the Guadalupe Dunes Oil Spill." *Social Problems* 49, no. 2 (2002): 50–177.

Beder, Sharon. *Power Play: The Fight to Control the World's Electricity.* New York: New Press, 2003.

Berardi, Gigi. "Natural Resource Policy, Unforgiving Geographies, and Persistent Poverty in Alaska Native Villages." *Natural Resources Journal* 38, no. 1 (1998): 85–108.

Bielawski, Ellen. "Inuit Indigenous Knowledge and Science in the Arctic." In *Naked Science: Anthropological Inquiry into Boundaries, Power, and Knowledge*, edited by Laura Nader, 216–227. New York: Routledge, 1996.

Blackburn, Robin. "The Enron Debacle and the Pension Crisis." *New Left Review* 14, no. 2 (2002).

Bolin, Bert and Erik Eriksson. "Changes in the Carbon Dioxide Content of the Atmosphere and Sea Due to Fossil Fuel Combustion." In *The Atmosphere and the Sea in Motion: Scientific Contributions to the Rossby Memorial Volume*, edited by Bert Bolin and Erik Eriksson, 130–142. New York: Rockefeller Institute Press, 1959.

Borneman, Walter R. *Alaska: Saga of a Bold Land*. New York: Harper Perennial, 2004.

Bowen, Mark. *Thin Ice: Unlocking the Secrets of Climate in the World's Highest Mountains*. New York: Owl Books, 2005.

Bowker, Michael. *Fatal Deception: The Untold Story of Asbestos: Why It Is Still Legal and Still Killing Us*. New York: Rodale Press, 2003.

Boykoff, Maxwell T. and Jules M. Boykoff. "Bias as Balance: Global Warming and the U.S. Prestige Press." *Global Environmental Change* 14, no. 2 (2004): 125–136.

Bradsher, Keith. *High and Mighty: SUVs—the World's Most Dangerous Vehicles and How They Got That Way*. Cambridge, MA: Perseus Books, 2002.

Breakthrough Institute. "Case Studies in American Innovation: A New Look at Government Involvement in Technological Development." Breakthrough Institute: Oakland, CA, April 2009.

Brodeur, Paul. *Outrageous Misconduct: The Asbestos Industry on Trial*. New York: Pantheon Books, 1985.

Broecker, Wallace S. and Robert Kunzig. *Fixing Climate: What Past Climate Changes Reveal about the Current Threat—and How to Counter It*. New York: Hill and Wang, 2009.

Brown, Caroline L. "Political and Legal Status of Alaska Natives." In *A Companion to the Anthropology of American Indians*, edited by Thomas Biolsi. Oxford: Blackwell Publishing, 2004.

Bullard, Robert D. *Confronting Environmental Racism: Voices from the Grassroots*. Cambridge, MA: South End Press, 1993.

Burch, Ernest S. Jr. "The Inupiat and the Christianization of Arctic Alaska." *Etudes/Inuit/Studies* 18, nos. 1–2 (1994): 81.

———. *Social Life in Northwest Alaska: The Structure of Inupiaq Eskimo Nations*. Fairbanks: University of Alaska Press, 2006.

Campbell, Colin J. and Jean H. Laherrére. "The End of Cheap Oil." *Scientific American* 278, no. 3 (1998): 60–65.

Carroll, Stephen J. *Asbestos Litigation*. Santa Monica, CA: Rand Corporation, 2005.

Case, David and Dalee Sambo Dorough. "Tribes and Self-Determination in Alaska." *Human Rights: Journal of the Section of Individual Rights & Responsibilities* 33, no. 2 (2006): 13–14.

Castleman, Barry I. *Asbestos: Medical and Legal Aspects*. New York: Aspen Publishers, 1986.

Center for Responsive Politics. "James M. Inhofe: Industry Data." March 27, 1011. www.opensecrets.org/politicians/industries.php?cycle=Career&cid=N0000558.

Chance, Norman A. *The Iñupiat and Arctic Alaska: An Ethnography of Development*. Fort Worth, TX: Holt Rinehart & Winston, 1990.

———. "Modernization and Educational Reform in Native Alaska." *Rethinking Modernization: Anthropological Perspectives*, 1974, 332.

Chandler, Alfred D. Jr. "The Beginnings of Big Business in American Industry." *Business History Review*, 1959, 1–31.

Checker, Melissa. *Polluted Promises: Environmental Racism and the Search for Justice in a Southern Town*. New York: NYU Press, 2005.

Chua, Peter, Kum-Kum Bhavnani, and John Foran. "Women, Culture, Development: A New Paradigm for Development Studies?" *Ethnic and Racial Studies* 23, no. 5 (2000): 820–841.

Churchill, Ward. *Struggle for the Land: Native North American Resistance to Genocide, Ecocide, and Colonization*. New York: City Lights Books, 2002.

Clark, William R. *Petrodollar Warfare: Oil, Iraq and the Future of the Dollar*. Gabriola Island, BC: New Society Publishers, 2005.

Clarke, Lee. "Considering Katrina." In *The Sociology of Katrina: Perspectives on a Modern Catastrophe*, edited by David L. Brunsma, David Overfelt, and J. Steve Picou, 236–241. Lanham, MD: Rowman and Littlefield, 2007.

CO2now.org, "Current Data for Atmospheric CO2." http://co2now.org/Current-CO2/CO2-Now/Current-Data-for-Atmospheric-CO2.html.

Cole, Luke and Sheila Foster. *From the Ground Up: Environmental Racism and the Rise of the Environmental Justice Movement*. New York: NYU Press, 2001.

Commission for Racial Justice and United Church of Christ. *Toxic Wastes and Race in the U.S.: A National Report on the Racial and Socio-Economic Characteristics of Communities with Hazardous Waste Sites*. New York: Public Data Access Inc., 1987.

Cook, Christopher D. "Coal Miners Slaughter." *In These Times*. January 25, 2006.

Cooper, Christopher and Robert J. Block. *Disaster: Hurricane Katrina and the Failure of Homeland Security*. New York: Owl Books, 2006.

Corbett, Julia B. and Jessica L. Durfee. "Testing Public (Un)Certainty of Science: Media Representations of Global Warming." *Science Communication* 26, no. 2 (2004): 129.

Costanza, Robert, et al. "The Value of the World's Ecosystem Services and Natural Capital." *Ecological Economics* 25, no. 1 (1998): 3–15.

Covington and Burling. "Tort Reform Project Budget." 1995. Philip Morris Bates No. 2047648299/8307.

Cranor, Carl F. *Toxic Torts: Science, Law, and the Possibility of Justice*. Cambridge: Cambridge University Press, 2006.

Cronon, William, George Miles, and Jay Gitlin, eds. *Under an Open Sky: Rethinking America's Western Past*. New York: W. W. Norton & Co., 1994.

Cushman, John H. "Industrial Group Plans to Battle Climate Treaty." *New York Times*. April 26, 1998.

Darlington, David. "Kivalina, Alaska: A Melting Village." *Reader's Digest*. October 2008.

Davis, Ann. "Morgan Stanley Trades Energy Old-Fashioned Way: In Barrels." *Wall Street Journal*. March 2, 2005.

Daynard, Richard A. "Tobacco Liability Litigation as a Cancer Control Strategy." *Journal of the National Cancer Institute* 80, no. 1 (1988): 9–13.

Deffeyes, Kenneth S. *Hubbert's Peak: The Impending World Oil Shortage*. Princeton, NJ: Princeton University Press, 2001.

Denworth, Lydia. *Toxic Truth: A Scientist, a Doctor, and the Battle over Lead*. Boston, MA: Beacon Press, 2009.

Derickson, Alan. *Black Lung: Anatomy of a Public Health Disaster*. Ithaca, NY: Cornell University Press, 1998.

Dickinson, Tim. "Obama's Sheriff." *Rolling Stone*. June 10, 2010.

Diehl, Harold S. *Tobacco & Your Health: The Smoking Controversy*. Columbus, OH: McGraw-Hill, 1969.

Donaghy, Timothy, et al. *Atmosphere of Pressure: Political Interference in Federal Climate Science*. A report of the Union of Concerned Scientists and the Government Accountability Project. Cambridge, MA: UCS Publications, 2007.

Doyle, Timothy and Melissa Risely. *Crucible for Survival: Environmental Justice and Security in the Indian Ocean Region*. New York: Rutgers University Press, 2007.

Duhigg, Charles. "Cleansing the Air at the Expense of Waterways." *New York Times*. October 12, 2009.

Dumanoski, Dianne. *The End of the Long Summer: Why We Must Remake Our Civilization to Survive on a Volatile Earth*. New York: Crown Books, 2009.

Edwards, Wayne and Tara Natarajan. "ANCSA and ANILCA: Capabilities Failure?" *Native Studies Review* 17, no. 2 (2008): 69.

Energy Information Administration. "The Changing Structure of the Electric Power Industry 2000: An Update." October 2000. www.eia.doe.gov/cneaf/electricity/chg_stru_update/toc.html.

———. "Greenhouse Gases, Climate Change, and Energy." April 2, 2004. www.eia.doe.gov/bookshelf/brochures/greenhouse/Chapter1.htm.

———. "Major U.S. Coal Producers, 2008." Released 2009. www.eia.doe.gov/cneaf/coal/page/acr/table10.html.

———. "U.S. Coal Exports: Data for October–December (4th Quarter 2009)." Report released March 2010. www.eia.doe.gov/cneaf/coal/quarterly/html/t7p01p1.html.

Environmental Protection Agency. "Control of Emissions from New Highway Vehicles and Engines." Notice of denial of petition for rulemaking. FRL-7554-7. *Federal Register* 68, no. 173 (September 8, 2003): 52925.

———. "Executive Summary: 2009 U.S. Greenhouse Inventory Report." In *Inventory of U.S. Greenhouse Gas Emissions and Sinks, 1990–2007*. Washington, DC: Environmental Protection Agency, 2009.

———. "Mountaintop Mining/Valley Fills in Appalachia: Final Programmatic Environmental Impact Statement—2005." Updated February 11, 2011. www.epa.gov/Region3/mtntop/eis2005.htm.

Epstein, Lois N., Stephen Greetham, and Anaa Karuba. *Ranking Refineries: What Do We Know about Oil Refinery Pollution from Right-to-Know Data*. Washington, DC: Environmental Defense Fund, 1995.

Epstein, Paul R. and Jesse Selber. *Oil: A Life Cycle Analysis of Its Health and Environmental Impacts*. Boston, MA: Center for Health and the Global Environment, Harvard Medical School, 2002.

Epstein, Paul R., et al. "Full Cost Accounting for the Life Cycle of Coal." *Annals from the New York Academy of Sciences* 1219 (2011): 73–98, http://onlinelibrary.wiley.com/doi/10.1111/j.1749-6632.2010.05890.x/pdf.

Erikson, Kai. "Disaster at Buffalo Creek: Loss of Communality at Buffalo Creek." *American Journal of Psychiatry* 133, no. 3 (1976): 302.

Ewick, Patricia and Susan S. Silbey. "Conformity, Contestation, and Resistance: An Account of Legal Consciousness." *New England Law Review* 26 (1991): 731.

Faris, Stephen. "The Real Roots of Darfur." *Atlantic Monthly* 299, no. 3 (April 2007): 67–69.

Fischer, Henry W. *Response to Disaster: Fact versus Fiction & Its Perpetuation.* Lanham, MD: University Press of America, 1998.

Fishback, Price V. and Shawn Everett Kantor. *A Prelude to the Welfare State: The Origins of Workers' Compensation.* Chicago: University of Chicago Press, 2006.

Fisher, Dana R. "Bringing the Material Back In: Understanding the US Position on Climate Change." *Sociological Forum* 21, no. 3 (2006): 467–494.

Flannery, Tim. *The Weather Makers: How Man Is Changing the Climate and What It Means for Life on Earth.* New York: Grove Press, 2006.

Fleming, James R. *Historical Perspectives on Climate Change.* Oxford: Oxford University Press on Demand, 2005.

Foucault, Michel. *Discipline and Punish: The Birth of the Prison.* New York: Vintage Books, 1995.

Fox, Josh. *Gasland.* New York: HBO Documentary Films, 2010.

Frank, Andre Gunder. "The Development of Underdevelopment." In *The Sustainable Urban Development Reader*, edited by Timothy Beatley and Stephen M. Wheeler. New York: Routledge, 2004.

Freudenburg, William R. "Privileged Access, Privileged Accounts: Toward a Socially Structured Theory of Resources and Discourses." *Social Forces* 84 (2005): 89–114.

———. "Social Constructions and Social Constrictions: Toward Analyzing the Social Construction of 'the Naturalized' as Well as 'the Natural.'" In *Environment and Global Modernity*, edited by G. Spaargaren, A. Mol, and F. Buttel. London: Sage Press, 2000.

Freudenburg, William R., et al. *Catastrophe in the Making: The Engineering of Katrina and the Disasters of Tomorrow.* Washington, DC: Island Press, 2009.

Freudenburg, William and Robert Gramling. *Oil in Troubled Waters: Perceptions, Politics, and the Battle over Offshore Drilling.* Albany: SUNY Press, 1994.

———. "Bureaucratic Slippage and Failures of Agency Vigilance: The Case of the Environmental Studies Program." *Social Problems* 41, no. 2 (1994): 214–239.

Freudenburg, William R., Robert Gramling, and D. J. Davidson. "Scientific Certainty Argumentation Methods (SCAMs): Science and the Politics of Doubt." *Sociological Inquiry* 78, no. 1 (2008): 2–38.

Freudenburg, William R. and Lisa J. Wilson. "Mining the Data: Analyzing the Socioeconomic Effects of Mining on Rural Communities." *Sociological Inquiry* 72, no. 4 (2002): 549–575.

Friedman, L. C. "Tobacco Industry Use of Judicial Seminars to Influence Rulings in Products Liability Litigation." *Tobacco Control* 15, no. 2 (2006): 120–124.

Friedman, L. C., Richard Daynard, and Christopher N. Banthin. "How Tobacco-Friendly Science Escapes Scrutiny in the Courtroom." *American Journal of Public Health* 95, suppl. 1 (2005): 16–20.

Fritschler, A. Lee. *Tobacco and Politics.* Englewood Cliffs, NJ: Prentice-Hall, 1989.

Fritz, Charles E. "Disaster." In *Contemporary Social Problems*, edited by Robert Merton and

Robert Nisbet, 651–694. New York: Harcourt, Brace, and World, 1961.

Fusaro, Peter and Gary M. Vasey. *Energy and Environmental Hedge Funds: The New Investment Paradigm.* San Francisco, CA: Wiley Publishing, 2006.

Fusaro, Peter and Jeremy Wilcox. *Energy Derivatives: Trading Emerging Markets.* New York: Energy Publishing Enterprises, 2000.

Gagliardi, Mark. "Stirring the Debate in Rhode Island: Should Lead Paint Manufacturers Be Held Liable for the Harm Caused by Lead Paint?" *Roger Williams University Law Review,* 2002, 341.

Galanter, Marc. "Why the Haves Come Out Ahead: Speculations on the Limits of Legal Change." *Law & Society Review* 9 (1974): 95.

Galanter, Marc and Thomas Palay. *Tournament of Lawyers: The Transformation of the Big Law Firm.* Chicago: University of Chicago Press, 1991.

Gedicks, Al. *Resource Rebels: Native Challenges to Mining and Oil Corporations.* Cambridge, MA: South End Press, 2001.

Gelbspan, Ross. *The Heat Is On: The Climate Crisis, the Cover-Up, the Prescription.* Cambridge, MA: Perseus Books, 1998.

Gellman, Barton. *Angler: The Cheney Vice Presidency.* New York: Penguin Press, 2008.

Gibney, Alex, Bethany McLean, and Peter Elkind. *Enron: The Smartest Guys in the Room.* Directed by Alex Gibney. New York: Magnolia Pictures, 2005.

Gifford, Donald G. "Public Nuisance as a Mass Products Liability Tort." *University of Cincinnati Law Review* 71 (2003): 741–837.

Glantz, Stanton A. *The Cigarette Papers.* Berkeley and Los Angeles: University of California Press, 1996.

Goodell, Jeff. *Big Coal: The Dirty Secret behind America's Energy Future.* New York: Houghton Mifflin, 2007.

———. "Secretary of Saving the Planet." *Rolling Stone.* June 25, 2009.

Gordon, J. "Inter-American Commission on Human Rights to Hold Hearing after Rejecting Inuit Climate Change Petition." *Sustainable Develeopment Law & Policy* 7 (2006): 55.

Gotham, Kevin Fox and Miriam Greenberg. "From 9/11 to 8/29: Post-Disaster Recovery and Rebuilding in New York and New Orleans." *Social Forces* 87, no. 2 (2008): 1039–1062.

Government Accountability Office. *Alaska Native Villages: Limited Progress Has Been Made on Relocating Villages Threatened by Flooding and Erosion.* Report GAO-09-551. Washington, DC: Government Accountability Office, June 2009.

———. *Alaska Native Villages: Most Are Affected by Flooding and Erosion, but Few Qualify for Federal Assistance.* Report GAO-04-142. Washington, DC: Government Accountability Office, 2003.

———. "Coal Power Plants: Opportunities Exist for DOE to Provide Better Information on the Maturity of Key Technologies to Reduce Carbon Dioxide Emissions." Report to Congressional Requesters, June 2010. www.gao.gov/new.items/d10675.pdf.

Graebner, William. "Hegemony through Science: Information Engineering and Lead Toxicology, 1925–1965," in *Dying for Work: Workers' Safety and Health in Twentieth-Century America,* edited by David Rosner and Gerald Markowitz, 140–59. Bloomington: Indiana University Press, 1987.

Gramling, Robert and William R. Freudenburg. "The Exxon Valdez Oil Spill in the Context of US Petroleum Politics." *Organization & Environment* 6, no. 3 (1992): 175.

Grant, John. *Corrupted Science: Fraud, Ideology, and Politics in Science.* Wisley, UK: FF&F Publishers, 2007.

Greenpeace. *Koch Industries: Secretly Funding the Climate Denial Machine.* Washington, DC: Greenpeace USA, March 2010.

Grossman, Richard L. and Frank T. Adams. *Taking Care of Business: Citizenship and the Charter of Incorporation.* Cambridge, MA: Charter, Ink, 1993

Guardino, Sara D. and Richard A. Daynard, "Tobacco Industry Lawyers as 'Disease Vectors.'" *British Medical Journal* 16, no. 4 (2007): 224–228.

Hamilton, Clive. *Scorcher: The Dirty Politics of Climate Change.* Melbourne, Australia: Black Inc., 2007.

Hansen, Art and Anthony Oliver-Smith. *Involuntary Migration and Resettlement: The Problems and Responses of Dislocated People.* Boulder, CO: Westview Press, 1982.

Hansen, Evan and Margaret Janes. *Coal Mining and the Clean Water Act: Why Regulated Coal Mines Still Pollute West Virginia's Streams.* Elkins, WV: West Virginia Rivers Coalition and Appalachian Center for the Economy and the Environment. April 2003.

Hansen, James, et al. "Climate Impact of Increasing Atmospheric Carbon Dioxide." *Science* 213, no. 4511 (1981): 957–966.

———. *Storms of My Grandchildren: The Truth about the Coming Climate Catastrophe and Our Last Chance to Save Humanity.* London: Bloomsbury Publishing, 2009.

Hardt, Michael and Antonio Negri. *Empire.* Cambridge, MA: Harvard University Press, 2001.

Hartmann, Thom. *Unequal Protection: The Rise of Corporate Dominance and the Theft of Human Rights.* New York: Rodale Books, 2002.

Haycox, Stephen. *Alaska: An American Colony.* Seattle: University of Washington Press, 2006.

Helvarg, David. *Blue Frontier: Saving America's Living Seas.* New York: Owl Books, 2001.

Henson, Robert. *The Rough Guide to Climate Change.* New York: Penguin Group, 2006.

Hewitt, Kenneth. *Interpretations of Calamity.* Winchester, MA: Allen & Unwin, 1983.

Hirsch, Richard F. *Power Loss: The Origins of Deregulation and Restructuring in the American Electric Utility System.* Cambridge, MA: MIT Press, 1999.

Hirsch, Robert L., et al. *Peaking of World Oil Production: Impacts, Mitigation, & Risk Management.* Washington, DC: U.S. Department of Energy, National Energy Technology Laboratory (NETL), February 2005.

Hirt, Paul W. *A Conspiracy of Optimism: Management of the National Forests since World War Two.* Lincoln: University of Nebraska Press, 1994.

Houghton, John T., Gregory Jenkins, and J. J. Ephraums, eds. *Executive Summary on Climate Change for Policymakers.* Report of the Intergovernmental Panel on Climate Change. Cambridge: Cambridge University Press.

Huber, Peter. *Galileo's Revenge: Junk Science in the Courtroom.* New York: Basic Books, 1993.

Intergovernmental Panel on Climate Change. "The Science of Climate Change." In *IPCC Second Assessment 1995.* Report of the Intergovernmental Panel on Climate Change. Geneva, Switzerland: IPCC, December 1995.

Jacques, Peter J., Riley E. Dunlap, and Mark Freeman. "The Organisation of Denial: Conservative Think Tanks and Environmental Scepticism." *Environmental Politics* 17, no. 3 (2008): 349–385.

Janutis, Rachel M. "The Struggle over Tort Reform and the Overlooked Legacy of the Progressives." *Akron Law Review* 39 (2006): 943.

Jarecki, Eugene. *Why We Fight.* New York: Sony Pictures, 2005.

Johnson, Chalmers. *Blowback: The Costs and Consequences of American Empire.* New York: Owl Books, 2004.

Johnson, James P. *The Politics of Soft Coal: The Bituminous Industry from World War I through the New Deal.* Urbana-Champaign: University of Illinois Press, 1979.

Johnson, Rebecca L. *Investigating Climate Change: Scientists' Search for Answers in a Warming World.* Breckenridge, CO: Twenty-First Century Books. 2008.

Juhasz, Antonia. *The Tyranny of Oil.* New York: HarperCollins, 2008.

Kazis, Richard and Richard L. Grossman. *Fear at Work: Job Blackmail, Labor and the Environment.* New York: Pilgrim Press, 1982.

Keeton, W. Page, et al., eds. *Prosser and Keeton on the Law of Torts.* 5th ed. St. Paul, MN: West Publishing Co., 1984.

Kelder, Graham E. Jr. and Richard A. Daynard. "Judicial Approaches to Tobacco Control: The Third Wave of Tobacco Litigation as a Tobacco Control Mechanism." *Journal of Social Issues* 53, no. 1 (1997): 169–186.

Kelley, Ingrid N. *Energy in America: A Tour of Our Fossil Fuel Culture and Beyond.* Lebanon, NH: University Press of New England, 2008.

Kennedy, Robert F. Jr. *Crimes against Nature.* New York: HarperCollins, 2005.

Kintisch, Eli. "Global Warming: Projections of Climate Change Go from Bad to Worse, Scientists Report." *Science* 323, no. 5921 (2009): 1546–7.

Klare, Michael T. *Blood and Oil: The Dangers and Consequences of America's Growing Dependency on Imported Petroleum.* New York: Holt Paperbacks, 2005.

Klein, Naomi. "James Baker's Double Life." *Nation.* November 1, 2004.

———. *The Shock Doctrine: The Rise of Disaster Capitalism.* New York: Metropolitan Books, 2007.

Kluger, Richard. *Ashes to Ashes: America's Hundred-Year Cigarette War, the Public Health, and the Unabashed Triumph of Philip Morris.* New York: Vintage Books, 1996.

Koenig, Thomas H. "Crimtorts: A Cure for Hardening of the Categories." *Widener Law Journal* 17 (2008): 733–781.

Koenig, Thomas H. and Michael Rustad. "Crimtorts as Corporate Just Deserts." *University of Michigan Journal of Law Reform* 31 (1997): 289.

———. "Toxic Torts, Politics, and Environmental Justice: The Case for Crimtorts." *Law & Policy* 26, no. 2 (2004): 189–207.

Kolbert, Elizabeth. *Field Notes from a Catastrophe.* New York: Bloomsbury, 2006.

Kraft, Michael E. and Denise Scheberle, "Environmental Justice and the Allocation of Risk: The Case of Lead and Public Health." *Policy Studies Journal* 23, no. 1 (1995).

Kramer, Andrew. "Deals with Iraq Are Set to Bring Oil Giants Back." *New York Times.* June 19, 2008.

Kroll-Smith, J. Stephen, Phil Brown, and Valerie J. Gunter. *Illness and the Environment: A*

Reader in Contested Medicine. New York: NYU Press, 2000.

Krosnick, Jon A., Alysson L. Holbrook, and Penny S. Visser. "The Impact of the Fall 1997 Debate about Global Warming on American Public Opinion." *Public Understanding of Science* 9, no. 3 (2000): 239–260.

Kubasek, Nancy K. and Gary S. Silverman. *Environmental Law.* 5th ed. Englewood Cliffs, NJ: Prentice Hall, 2006.

———. *Environmental Law.* 6th ed. Englewood Cliffs, NJ: Prentice Hall, 2008.

Larsen, Bjorn and Anwar Shah. *World Fossil Fuel Subsidies and Global Carbon Emissions.* Background paper for World Development Report 1992. Washington, DC: Policy Research Dissemination Center, 1992.

Lauman, Edward O. and David Knoke. *The Organizational State: Social Change in National Policy Domains.* Madison: University of Wisconsin Press, 1987.

Lavell, Allan. "Decision Making and Risk Management." Presented at the Conference for Furthering Cooperation in Science and Technology for Caribbean Development. Port of Spain, Trinidad. September 25, 1998. www.la-red.org/public/articulos/1998/dmrm/dmrm1998_mar-1-2002.pdf.

Leggett, Jeremy K. *The Carbon War: Global Warming and the End of the Oil Era.* New York: Routledge, 2001.

———. *Half Gone: Oil, Gas, Hot Air and the Global Energy Crisis.* New York: Portobello Books, 2005.

LexisNexis, "The LexisNexis Special Report: The Rhode Island Lead Lawsuit." 2008. www.lexisnexis.com/Lead_Litigation.aspx.

Lipartito, Kenneth and Joseph A. Pratt, *Baker & Botts in the Development of Modern Houston.* Austin: University of Texas Press, 1991.

Little, Amanda. *Power Trip: From Oil Wells to Solar Cells—Our Ride to the Renewable Future.* New York: HarperCollins, 2009.

Lockwood, Mike and Claus Fröhlich. "Recent Oppositely Directed Trends in Solar Climate Forcings and the Global Mean Surface Air Temperature." *Proceedings of the Royal Society A: Mathematical, Physical and Engineering Sciences* 463, no. 2086 (2007): 2447.

Lorenzoni, Irene, Nick F. Pidgeon, and Robert E. O'Connor. "Dangerous Climate Change: The Role for Risk Research." *Risk Analysis* 25, no. 6 (2005): 1387–1398.

Losos, Elizabeth, et al. "Taxpayer-Subsidized Resource Extraction Harms Species." *BioScience* (1995): 446–455.

Lott, John. "Why You Should Be Hot and Bothered about 'Climategate.'" FoxNews.com. November 24, 2009. www.foxnews.com/opinion/2009/11/24/john-lott-climate-change-emails-copenhagen/.

MacCleery, Laura. *Safeguards at Risk: John Graham and Corporate America's Back Door to the Bush White House.* Washington, DC: Public Citizen, 2001.

Magrath, C. Peter. *Morrison R. Waite: The Triumph of Character.* New York: Macmillan Books, 1963.

Mank, Bradford C. "Standing and Global Warming: Is Injury to All Injury to None?" *Environmental Law* 35, no. 1 (2005): 1–85.

Markowitz, Gerald and David Rosner. "'Cater to the Children': The Role of the Lead Industry in a Public Health Tragedy, 1900–1955." *American Journal of Public Health* 90, no.

1 (2000): 36–46.

———. "The Limits of Thresholds: Silica and the Politics of Science, 1935 to 1990." *American Journal of Public Health* 85, no. 2 (1995): 253–262.

Mather, Lynn. "Theorizing about Trial Courts: Lawyers, Policymaking, and Tobacco Litigation." *Law & Social Inquiry* 23, no. 4 (1998): 897–940.

Mayer, Jane. "Covert Operations: The Billionaire Brothers Who Are Waging a War against Obama." *New Yorker*. August 30, 2010.

McCright, Aaron M. and Riley E. Dunlap. "Challenging Global Warming as a Social Problem: An Analysis of the Conservative Movement's Counter-Claims." *Social Problems*, 2000, 499–522.

———. "Defeating Kyoto: The Conservative Movement's Impact on US Climate Change Policy." *Social Problems* 50, no. 3 (2003): 348–373.

McCulloch, Jock and Geoffrey Tweedale, *Defending the Indefensible: The Global Asbestos Industry and Its Fight for Survival*. New York: Oxford University Press, 2008.

McDonald, Forrest. *Insull: The Rise and Fall of a Billionaire Utility Tycoon*. New York: Beard Books, 2004.

Mercer, David and Gary Edmond. "Daubert and the Exclusionary Ethos: The Convergence of Corporate and Judicial Attitudes Towards the Admissibility of Expert Evidence in Tort Litigation." *Law & Policy* 26, no. 2 (2004): 231–257.

Meyers, William. *The Santa Clara Blues: Corporate Personhood Versus Democracy*. Gualala, CA: III Publishing, 2001.

Michaels, David. *Doubt Is Their Product: How Industry's Assault on Science Threatens Your Health*. Oxford: Oxford University Press, 2008.

Miller, Karen S. *The Voice of Business: Hill & Knowlton and Postwar Public Relations*. Chapel Hill: University of North Carolina Press, 1999.

Mitchell, Janet. "Erosion." City of Kivalina website. 2007. www.kivalinacity.com.

———. "Relocation." City of Kivalina website. 2007. www.kivalinacity.com.

Mohai, Paul and Bunyan Bryant. "Environmental Racism: Reviewing the Evidence." In *Race and the Incidence of Environmental Hazards: A Time for Discourse*, edited by Paul Mohai and Bunyan Bryant, 163–76. Boulder, CO: Westview Press, 1992.

Mollenkamp, Carrick. *The People vs. Big Tobacco: How the States Took On the Cigarette Giants*. New York: Bloomberg Press, 1998.

Molotch, Harvey. "Oil in Santa Barbara and Power in America." *Sociological Inquiry* 40, no. 1 (1970): 131–144.

Monbiot, George. *Heat: How to Stop the Planet from Burning*. London: Penguin Books, 2007.

Monirul Qader Mirza, M. "Global Warming and Changes in the Probability of Occurrence of Floods in Bangladesh and Implications." *Global Environmental Change* 12, no. 2 (2002): 127–138.

Monks, Robert A. G. and Nell Minow. *Watching the Watchers: Corporate Governance for the 21st Century*. Oxford: Blackwell Publishing, 1996.

Mooney, Chris. *Republican War on Science*. Cambridge, MA: Basic Books, 2006.

———. *Storm World: Hurricanes, Politics, and the Battle over Global Warming*. New York: Harvest Books, 2008.

MSNBC, "Nixon Administration Debated Global Warming," July 3, 2010, www.msnbc
.msn.com/id/38070412/ns/politics.

Nace, Ted. *Climate Hope: On the Front Lines of the Fight against Coal.* San Francisco, CA:
CoalSwarm, 2009. www.sourcewatch.org/index.php?title=Climate_Hope.

———. *Gangs of America: The Rise of Corporate Power and the Disabling of Democracy.* New
York: Berrett-Koehler Publishers, 2005.

Nader, Ralph and Wesley J. Smith. *No Contest: Corporate Lawyers and the Perversion of Justice
in America.* New York: Random House, 1996.

National Assessment Synthesis Team, U.S. Global Change Research Program. *Climate Change
Impacts on the United States: The Potential Consequences of Climate Variability and Change.
Overview: Alaska.* Washington, DC: U.S. Global Change Research Program, 2000.

Newell, Peter. *Climate for Change: Non-State Actors and the Global Politics of the Greenhouse.*
Cambridge: Cambridge University Press, 2000.

Northwest Arctic Native Association, "About Kivalina." NANA website. 2010. www.nana.com/
regional/about-us/overview-of-region/kivalina/.

Novick, Sheldon. "The Electric Power Industry." *Environment* 17, no. 8 (1975).

O'Brien, David M. *Storm Center: The Supreme Court in American Politics.* New York: W. W.
Norton & Co., 1996.

Odell, Peter R. *Oil and World Power.* Middlesex, UK: Penguin Books, 1983.

Office of the Assistant Secretary of Defense for Reserve Affairs. "Support and Services for
Eligible Organizations and Activities outside the Department of Defense: Terms and
Conditions." Innovative Readiness Training Guidelines, 1997. http://irt.defense.gov/
about.html.

Olson, Paul A. *The Struggle for the Land.* Lincoln: University of Nebraska Press, 1990.

Olthuis, Diane. *It Happened in Alaska.* New York: Globe Pequot Press, 2006.

O'Neill, Dan. "Frozen in Time." *National Parks* 81 (Spring 2007): 24–30.

———. *Last Giant of Beringia: The Mystery of the Bering Land Bridge.* New York: Basic
Books, 2005.

———. *The Firecracker Boys.* New York: St. Martin's Press, 1994.

Oreskes, Naomi. "Beyond the Ivory Tower: The Scientific Consensus on Climate Change."
Science 306, no. 5702 (2004): 1686.

———. "Science and Public Policy: What's Proof Got to Do with It?" *Environmental Science
and Policy* 7, no. 5 (2004): 369–383.

Oreskes, Naomi, Erik M. Conway, and Matthew Shindell. "From Chicken Little to Dr. Pangloss: William Nierenberg, Global Warming, and the Social Deconstruction of Scientific Knowledge." *Historical Studies in the Natural Sciences* 38, no. 1 (2008): 109–152.

Osborne, William A. "The History of Military Assistance for Domestic Natural Disasters:
The Return to a Primary Role for the Department of Defense in the Twenty-First
Century?" *Army Lawyer,* December 2006, 1.

Pace, Michael L. and Peter M. Groffman. *Successes, Limitations, and Frontiers in Ecosystem
Science.* New York: Springer-Verlag, 1998.

Pachauri, Rajendra K. and Andy Reisinger, eds. *Climate Change 2007: Synthesis Report.* Fourth
Assessment Report of the Intergovernmental Panel on Climate Change. Geneva, Swit-

zerland: IPCC, 2007.

Partnoy, Frank. *Infectious Greed: How Deceit and Risk Corrupted the Financial Markets*. New York: Owl Books, 2004.

Pearce, Fred. *With Speed and Violence: Why Scientists Fear Tipping Points in Climate Change*. Boston: Beacon Press, 2007.

Perillo, Lisa A. "Scraping Beneath the Surface: Finally Holding Lead-Based Paint Manufacturers Liable by Applying Public Nuisance and Market-Share Liability Theories." *Hofstra Law Review* 32 (2003): 1039.

Petit, Jean-Robert, et al. "Climate and Atmospheric History of the Past 420,000 Years from the Vostok Ice Core, Antarctica." *Nature* 399, no. 6735 (1999): 429–436.

Pew Charitable Trusts. *Who's Winning the Clean Energy Race? Growth, Competition, and Opportunity in the World's Largest Economies*. G-20 Clean Energy Factbook. Philadelphia, PA: Pew Charitable Trusts, 2010.

Phillips, Kevin. *American Dynasty: Aristocracy, Fortune, and the Politics of Deceit in the House of Bush*. New York: Viking Books, 2004.

———. *American Theocracy: The Peril and Politics of Radical Religion, Oil, and Borrowed Money in the 21st Century*. New York: Viking Books, 2006.

Pinter, Nicholas. "One Step Forward, Two Steps Back on U.S. Floodplains." *Science* 308, no. 5719 (2005): 207–208.

Pringle, Peter. "The Chronicles of Tobacco: An Account of the Forces That Brought the Tobacco Industry to the Negotiating Table." *William Mitchell Law Review* 25 (1999): 87.

Proctor, Robert N. Review of *Cancer Wars: How Politics Shapes What We Know and Don't Know about Cancer*, by Daniel M. Fox. *Bulletin of the History of Medicine* 71, no. 4 (1997): 747–748.

R. J. Reynolds Tobacco Company. "Tort Reform Project." January 1995. Legacy Tobacco Documents Library, University of California at San Francisco. http://legacy.library.ucsf.edu/tid/qpg30d00.

Rabin, Rick. "The Rhode Island Lead Paint Lawsuit: Where Do We Go from Here?" *New Solutions: A Journal of Environmental and Occupational Health Policy* 16, no. 4 (2006): 353–363.

Rampton, Sheldon and John Stauber, *Trust Us, We're Experts: How Industry Manipulates Science and Gambles with Your Future*. New York: Putnam, 2001.

Reardon, Jack. "Private Equity Firms and the Irrelevance of Traditional Monopoly." Presented at the Second Seminary of Heterodox Microeconomy, Universidad Nacional Autónoma de Mexico. October 2007.

Redfield, Alfred C. "The Biological Control of Chemical Factors in the Environment." *American Scientist* 46, no. 3 (1958): 205–221.

Redmond, Adrian. "The New Horizon," *The Native Experience*, episode 2. Skanderborg, Denmark: Channel 6 Television, 2001.

Reichman, Nancy. "Moving Backstage: Uncovering the Role of Compliance Practices in Shaping Regulatory Policy." In *White Collar Crime Reconsidered*, edited by Kip Schlegel and David Weisburg, 245–267. Boston: Northeastern University Press, 1992.

Revkin, Andrew. "Industry Ignored Its Scientists on Climate." *New York Times*. April 24, 2009.

Rich, Andrew and R. Kent Weaver. "Think Tanks in the U.S. Media." *Harvard International*

Journal of Press Politics 5, no. 4 (2000): 81–103.

Roberts, J. Timmons. "Global Inequality and Climate Change." *Society & Natural Resources* 14, no. 6 (2001): 501–509.

Roberts, Paul. *The End of Oil: On the Edge of a Perilous New World.* Boston, MA: Houghton Mifflin, 2004.

Robinson, William I. *Promoting Polyarchy: Globalization, U.S. Intervention, and Hegemony.* Cambridge: Cambridge University Press, 1996.

Roddick, Jacqueline. *The Dance of the Millions: Latin America and the Debt Crisis.* London: Latin America Bureau, 1988.

Rodhe, Henning, Robert Charlson, and Elizabeth Crawford. "Svante Arrhenius and the Greenhouse Effect." *Ambio* 26, no. 1 (1997): 2–5.

Rosen, Christine Meisner. "'Knowing' Industrial Pollution: Nuisance Law and the Power of Tradition in a Time of Rapid Economic Change, 1840–1864." *Environmental History* 8, no. 4 (2003): 565–597.

Rosner, David and Gerald Markowitz, "A 'Gift of God'?: The Public Health Controversy over Leaded Gasoline During the 1920s." *American Journal of Public Health* 75, no. 4 (1985): 344–352.

Rudolph, Richard, and Scott Ridley. *Power Struggle: The Hundred-Year War over Electricity.* New York: HarperCollins, 1986.

Sample, Ian. "Scientists Offered Cash to Dispute Climate Study," *Guardian* (UK). February 3, 2007.

Sampson, Anthony. *The Seven Sisters: The Great Oil Companies and the World They Made.* New York: Viking Books, 1975.

Sanjour, William. *Why EPA Is Like It Is and What Can Be Done about It.* Annapolis, MD: Environmental Research Foundation, 1992.

Sarat, Austin and Stuart A. Scheingold. *Cause Lawyering: Political Commitments and Professional Responsibilities.* New York: Oxford University Press, 1998.

Scahill, Jeremy. *Blackwater: The Rise of the World's Most Powerful Mercenary Army.* New York: Nation Books, 2008.

Schaeffer, Eric. "Junketing Judges: A Case of Bad Science." *Washington Post.* June 4, 2006.

Scherer, Michael. "Little Big Companies." *Mother Jones,* January–February 2005.

Schwartz, Victor E. and Phil Goldberg. "The Law of Public Nuisance: Maintaining Rational Boundaries on a Rational Tort." *Washburn Legal Journal* 45 (2005): 541.

Scott, Rachel. *Muscle and Blood.* New York: Dutton, 1974.

Selikoff, Irving J., Jacob Churg, and E. Cuyler Hammond. "Relation between Exposure to Asbestos and Mesothelioma." *New England Journal of Medicine* 272 (1965): 560.

Senate Committee on Homeland Security and Governmental Affairs. "The Role of Market Speculation in Rising Oil and Gas Prices: A Need to Put the Cop Back on the Beat." 109th Congress, 2nd session. U.S. Government Printing Office, Washington, DC: June 27, 2006. http://hsgac.senate.gov/public/_files/SenatePrint10965MarketSpecReportFINAL.pdf.

Silbey, Susan S. and Egon Bittner. "The Availability of Law." *Law & Policy* 4 (1982), 399.

Silverstein, K., *Smoke and Mirrors: The Tobacco Industry's Influence on the Phony 'Grassroots'*

Campaign for Liability Limits. Washington, DC: Public Citizen, 1996.

Simons, Kenneth W. "The Crime/Tort Distinction: Legal Doctrine and Normative Perspectives." *Widener Law Journal* 17 (2008): 719.

Sklar, Martin J. *The Corporate Reconstruction of American Capitalism, 1890–1916: The Market, the Law, and Politics.* Cambridge: Cambridge University Press, 1988.

Snider, Laureen. "Sociology of Corporate Crime." Theoretical Criminology 4 (2000): 169.

Solnit, Rebecca. *A Paradise Built in Hell: The Extraordinary Communities That Arise in Disaster.* New York: Penguin Group, 2009.

Spring, Joel H. *The Cultural Transformation of a Native American Family and Its Tribe 1763–1995.* Mahwah, NJ: Lawrence Erlbaum Associates, 1996.

Standlea, David M. *Oil, Globalization, and the War for the Arctic Refuge.* Albany, NY: SUNY Press, 2006.

Steinberg, Ted. *Acts of God: The Unnatural History of Natural Disaster in America.* Oxford: Oxford University Press, 2006.

Stiglitz, Joseph E. *Globalization and Its Discontents.* London: Allen Lane/Penguin Books, 2002.

Stone, Peter H. "Grassroots Group Rakes In the Green." *National Journal* 27 (March 11, 1995): 621.

Strohmeyer, John. *Extreme Conditions: Big Oil and the Transformation of Alaska.* New York: Simon & Schuster, 1993.

Taibbi, Matt. "The Great American Bubble Machine." *Rolling Stone.* July 9–23, 2009.

Tarbell, Ida M. *The History of the Standard Oil Company.* New York: McClure, Phillips & Co., 1904.

Templet, Paul H. "Grazing the Commons: An Empirical Analysis of Externalities, Subsidies and Sustainability." *Ecological Economics* 12, no. 2 (1995): 141–159.

Thompson, Carl Dean. *Confessions of the Power Trust.* New York: Arno Press, 1976.

Tickell, Joshua, Meghan Murphy, and Claudio Graziano. *Biodiesel America: How to Achieve Energy Security, Free America from Middle East Oil Dependence, and Make Money Growing Fuel.* Portland, OR: Yorkshire Press, 2006.

Tierney, Kathleen J. "Disaster Beliefs and Institutional Interests: Recycling Disaster Myths in the Aftermath of 9-11." *Research in Social Problems and Public Policy* 11 (2003): 33–51.

———. "Social Inequality, Hazards, and Disasters." In *On Risk and Disaster: Lessons from Hurricane Katrina,* edited by Ronald Joel Daniels, Donald F. Kettl, and Howard Kunreuther, 109–128. Philadelphia: University of Pennsylvania Press, 2006.

Tierney, Kathleen J., Michael K. Lindell, and Ronald W. Perry. *Facing the Unexpected: Disaster Preparedness and Response in the United States.* Washington, DC: National Academy Press, 2001.

Tipps, Peter. "Controlling the Lead Paint Debate: Why Control Is Not an Element of Public Nuisance." *Boston College Law Review* 50 (2009): 605–638.

Tucker, Eric. "Lead Paint Ruling Could Lead to More Lawsuits, Experts Say." *Boston Globe.* February 20, 2006.

Turka, Robert J. and Richard E. Gray. "Impacts of Coal Mining." *Humans as Geologic Agents* 16 (2005): 79.

U.S. Army Corps of Engineers. "Alaska Village Erosion Technical Assistance Program: An

Examination of Erosion Issues in the Communities of Bethel, Dillingham, Kaktovik, Kivalina, Newtok, Shishmaref, and Unalakleet." Army Corps of Engineers Report, April 2006. www.housemajority.org/coms/cli/AVETA_Report.pdf.

———. "Kivalina Relocation Master Plan Final Report." Army Corps of Engineers Report, June 2006. www.poa.usace.army.mil/en/cw/Kivalina/Kivalina.html.

———. "Section 117 Expedited Erosion Control Project for Kivalina, Alaska: Environmental Assessment and Finding of No Significant Impact." U.S. Army Corps of Engineers Environmental Assessment Report, September 2007.

Unger, Craig. *House of Bush, House of Saud: The Secret Relationship between the World's Two Most Powerful Dynasties*. New York: Scribner, 2004.

Union of Concerned Scientists. *Smoke, Mirrors, and Hot Air: How ExxonMobil Uses Big Tobacco's Tactics to Manufacture Uncertainty on Climate Science*. Cambridge, MA: UCS Publications, January 2007.

Vidal, John. "Revealed: How Oil Giant Influenced Bush." *Guardian* (UK). June 8, 2005.

Wall Street Journal. "The Tip of the Climategate Iceberg: The Global Warming Scandal Is Bigger Than One Email Leak." December 8, 2009.

Wallace-Wells, Benjamin. "Polar Fleeced." *Washington Monthly*, July–August 2005.

Weart, Spencer R. *The Discovery of Global Warming*. Cambridge, MA: Harvard University Press, 2008.

Weeks, James L. "Tampering with Dust Samples in Coal Mines (Again)." *American Journal of Industrial Medicine* 20, no. 2 (1991): 141–144.

Wells, Celia. *Corporations and Criminal Responsibility*. Oxford: Oxford University Press, 2001.

Wenger, Dennis E., et al. "It's a Matter of Myths: An Empirical Examination of Individual Insight into Disaster Response." In *Collective Behavior: A Source Book*, edited by M. Pugh. St. Paul, MN: West Publishing, 1980.

Wickham, J. D., et al. "The Effect of Appalachian Mountaintop Mining on Interior Forest." *Landscape Ecology* 22, no. 2 (2007): 79–187.

Wilkinson, Charles F. *Blood Struggle: The Rise of Modern Indian Nations*. New York: W. W. Norton & Co., 2005.

———. "Home Dance, the Hopi, and Black Mesa Coal: Conquest and Endurance in the American Southwest." *Brigham Young University Law Review* 2 (1996): 449–482.

Williams, Raymond. *Culture and Society 1780–1950*. New York: Columbia University Press, 1959.

Yergin, Daniel. *The Prize: The Epic Quest for Oil, Money, and Power*. New York: Simon & Schuster, 1991.

Zernike, Kate. "Secretive Republican Donors Are Planning Ahead." *New York Times*. October 20, 2010.

Zimring, Franklin. "Comparing Cigarette Policy and Illicit Drug and Alcohol Control." In *Smoking Policy: Law, Politics, and Culture*, edited by Robert Rabin and Stephen Sugarman. New York: Oxford University Press, 1993.

Zinn, Howard. *A People's History of the United States: 1492–Present*. New York: HarperCollins, 2003.

Cases Cited

Baker v. Carr, 369 U.S. 186 (1962)
California v. General Motors Corp., WL 2726871 (N.D. Cal. Sept. 17, 2007), dismissed
Castano v. American Tobacco, et al. (class action, U.S. Dist. Ct. E. LA, 1994), dismissed
Cipollone v. Liggett Group, Inc., 505 U.S. 504 (1992)
Citizens United v. Federal Election Commission, 558 U.S. ___ (2010)
City of Milwaukee v. Illinois, 451 U.S. 304 (1981)
City of St. Louis v. Benjamin Moore & Co., 226 S.W. 3d 110 (Mo. 2007)
Comer v. Murphy Oil Co., 1:05-CV-436 (S.D. Miss. Aug. 30, 2007), dismissed and appealed
Comer v. Murphy Oil Co., WL 3321493 (2009)
Connecticut v. American Electric Power Co., 406 F. Supp. 2d 265 (S.D.N.Y. 2005), dismissed
    and appealed
Connecticut v. American Electric Power Co., WL 2996729 (2009)
Daubert v. Merrell Dow Pharmaceuticals, 509 U.S. 579 (1993)
Haines v. Liggett Group, 814 F. Supp. 414 (D. N.J. 1993)
In re Lead Paint Litigation, 924 A.2d 484 (N.J. 2007)
Native Village of Kivalina v. ExxonMobil Corp., et al., C 08-1138 SBA, 12 (N.D. Cal. 2009),
    dismissed and appealed
Mass. v. EPA, 549 U.S. 497 (2007)
Mass. v. EPA, 415 F. 3d 50 (D.C. Cir. 2005), dismissed and appealed
Santa Clara County v. Southern Pacific Railroad Co., 118 U.S. 394 (1886)
State of Rhode Island v. Lead Industries Association, 951 A.2d 428 (R.I. 2008)

Interviews

Emma Adams, personal interview, August 9, 2008.
Enoch Adams, personal interview, August 8, 2008.
Russell Adams Jr., personal interview, August 9, 2008.
Andy Baldwin, personal interview, August 8, 2008.
Marilyn Baldwin, personal interview, August 9, 2008.
Steve Berman, personal interview, August 4, 2009.
Barry Castleman, personal interview, March 25, 2009.
Allen Chan, personal interview, July 28, 2009.
Luke Cole, personal interview, July 25, 2008.
David Frankson, personal interview, August 8, 2008.
Heather Kendall-Miller, personal interview, August 26, 2008, and August 18, 2009.
Ralph Knox, personal interview, August 8, 2009.
Gerald Markowitz, personal interview, March 18, 2009.
Bob McConnell, personal interview, May 28, 2009.
Jack McConnell, personal interview, May 27, 2009.
Mike McKinnon, personal interview, August 20, 2009.
David Michaels, personal interview, March 19, 2009.

Janet Mitchell, personal interview, August 25, 2008, and August 12, 2009.
Brent Newell, personal interview, August 3, 2009.
Patricia Opheen, personal interview, September 4, 2009.
David Rosner, personal interview, March 17, 2009.
Eric Schneider, personal interview, August 9, 2008.
Steve Susman, personal interview, May 2, 2009.
Colleen Swan, personal interview, August 7, 2008.
Dolly Swan, personal interview, August 8, 2008.
Joe Swan, personal interview, August 7, 2008.
Reppi Swan, personal interview, August 8, 2008.

INDEX

ABOUT THE AUTHOR

© Victoria Lawson

Christine Shearer is a researcher for CoalSwarm (part of SourceWatch) and the Center for Nanotechnology in Society at the University of California, Santa Barbara. She has previously worked at the KPFA Radio *Evening News*, the Center for Investigative Reporting, and the National Center for Ecological Analysis and Synthesis. Her work has appeared in academic and media publications including *Race, Gender & Class, Conservation Letters*, and *Newsweek*. She holds a PhD in sociology from UC Santa Barbara.